# NUMBERING
# IN AMERICAN
# SIGN LANGUAGE

Brenda E. Cartwright and Suellen J. Bahleda

**RID Press**
**Registry of Interpreters for the Deaf**
333 Commerce St, Alexandria, VA 22314
703.838.0030 (V), 703.838.0454 (FAX), 703.838.0459 (TTY)
www.rid.org

**Registry of Interpreters for the Deaf**

RID is a national membership organization representing the professionals who facilitate communication between people who are deaf or hard of hearing and people who can hear. Established in 1964 and incorporated in 1974, RID is a tax-exempt 501(c)(3) nonprofit organization.

It is the mission of RID to provide international, national, regional, state and local forums and an organizational structure for the continued growth and development of the profession of interpretation and transliteration of American Sign Language and English.

RID Press is the professional publishing arm of RID. The mission of RID Press is to extend the reach and reputation of RID through the publication of scholarly, practical, artistic and educational materials that advance the learning and knowledge of the profession of interpreting. The Press seeks to reflect the mission of RID by publishing a wide range of works that promote recognition and respect for the language and culture of deaf people and the practitioners in the field.

RID Press is a division of the Registry of Interpreters for the Deaf, 333 Commerce St, Alexandria, VA 22314, USA, (703) 838-0030, (703) 838-0459 TTY, www.rid.org

Published 2003

Library of Congress Control Number: 2002115164

ISBN 0-916883-35-3

Printed in the United States of America

# Contents

# ▶ Authors' Note

This book is the result of more than ten years of development, experimentation, and collaboration. Instructional approaches to counting and numeric incorporation have evolved over time with additional linguistic knowledge and insights into American Sign Language (ASL). This text has grown out of our need, as faculty members of ASL and interpreter programs, to better incorporate numbering systems into our curricula.

These instructional materials include drills and expressive and receptive activities. Our goal was to create a practical, useful, and comprehensive approach to teaching numbers and their variations across applications in ASL. The process of developing this text energized us and challenged us to evaluate our own instructional approaches and materials. We believe this book and its companion book, *Fingerspelling in American Sign Language,* capture that energy and will enhance numbering instruction across the spectrum, from beginning students to interpreters-in-training.

Our thanks to Deaf artist Mary Klein, who contributed the illustrations for this book. In addition, our gratitude and appreciation goes out to students, workshop participants, and esteemed colleagues who provided testing grounds and invaluable feedback over the years.

Brenda E. Cartwright, MS
CSC, CI and CT
Lansing Community College
Lansing, Michigan
BCartwright@lcc.edu

Suellen J. Bahleda, M.ED, M.DIV
CI and CT
University of Alaska Anchorage
Anchorage, Alaska
rwpress@juno.com

# ▶ Introduction

Learning to count is just the beginning of using numbering systems within ASL. Incorporating a wide range of numbering uses into practice is critical for your linguistic development. This text provides an informative, positive, and practical approach to numbering practice to help you learn numbering as an integral part of ASL, rather than an isolated component.

Your initial exposure to numbering and numbering systems, and how you incorporate numbers into practice, can greatly impact your attitude and ability to successfully use numbers in your own signing. This book provides a positive framework for learning numbering systems, with information and activities (expressive and receptive) for meaningful and fun practice.

# Unit One: Numbers 0–99

- ❖ **Preventing Repetitive Motion Injuries**
- ❖ **Overview**
- ❖ **Drill Practice Goals**
- ❖ **Drill:  Numbers 0–99**
- ❖ **Activities:  Things on the Tube**
                  **Around the Room**
                  **100 on the Dot**

# Preventing Repetitive Motion Injuries

ASL and interpreter programs can play an important role in preventing repetitive motion injuries (Stewart et al., 1988). Just as athletes warm up and increase their stamina in increments, so should signers and interpreters. You are encouraged to do warm-up stretches before numbering practice.

The following warm-up stretches can reduce the amount of stress the hand, wrist, arm, and shoulder receive while fingerspelling and signing. Each class session should begin with a variety of warm ups to limit potential cumulative trauma disorders. Warm-up stretches may be selected from the following:

## Warm-Up Exercises

**Shoulder Shrugs:** Slowly raise and drop shoulders several times.

**The Swan Dive:** Slowly stretch arms above your head until they meet, palms together. Gently lower them to shoulder level, palms up. Repeat.

**Finger Lifts:** Place hand palm down on a table or flat surface and slowly raise and lower each finger. Repeat with the other hand.

**Full Arm Stretch:** Hold arm out parallel to the floor, palm down. Lock elbow. Raise your hand so the fingertips point to the ceiling. With the other hand, gently press the raised fingers back toward your body for a five-count. Alternate with the other hand. Repeat twice.

**Palm Press:** Press palms together in front of your body. Keeping your elbows high, use the right palm to gently and slowly push the left palm backwards, from the wrist only, toward the left elbow. Slowly and gently, use the left palm to push the right palm backwards, from the wrist only, toward the right elbow. Repeat several times.

**The Frankenstein:** With arms stretched out in front of you, palms down, slowly open and close hands, stretching the fingers apart as far as possible. Repeat several times.

**Wrist Revolutions:** With closed hands, slowly rotate wrists in toward each other several times. Then rotate wrists away from each other several times.

# Overview

### Numbers 0–9

The palm faces out for 0, in for numbers 1–5, and out for 6–9 (see Appendix A). However, the palm faces out for 1–5 when they are in the "ones" position of a larger number (32, 64, 275, etc.).

### Numbers 16–19

There are variations for signing 16–19, although the most common method used is a combination sign: start with the "10" handshape (do not shake) and twist outward to the 6–9 position (10 + 6 = 16, 10 + 7 = 17, etc.).

### Decade Numbers

There is a specific sign for 20, while other "decade" numbers (30, 50, 80, etc.) are made by signing 3 + 0, 5 + 0, 8 + 0, and so on.

## Double Numbers

Double numbers (22, 33, 55, 77) are produced with the palm down, parallel to the floor. The number taps twice, moving from the center of the body out to the dominant side.

## Numbers 21–29

These numbers (except 22) use an "L" shape as the root, rather than the handshape "2."

## Numbers 23 and 25

These numbers have variants. They can be produced following the pattern described above (the "L" root + 3, the "L" root +5). A variant for 23 is to produce the number 3, palm out, and wiggle the middle finger. For 25, produce the number 5, palm out, and wiggle either the middle finger or both the middle finger and ring finger together.

## Numbers 67–69, 76–79 (excluding 77), 86–89 (excluding 88), and 96–98

These numbers incorporate specific movements for clarity. When the "tens" number is smaller than the "ones" (67, 78, 89), the first number is made away from the body, and the second number rocks toward the center of the body. When the "tens" number is larger than the "ones" (76, 86, 98), the first number is made at the center of the body, and the second number rocks away from the body.

# Drill Practice Goals

Numbering drills meet a number of practice goals:

- ■ Drills are used to build up and increase stamina. Focused practice on numbering can be physically demanding. Students should do warm-up exercises before beginning numbering practice.

- ■ Drills reinforce production of numbers as a whole within a context, rather than as a number-by-number string.

- ■ Drills reinforce the differences in numbering production based on context.

- ■ Drills assist in the development of rhythm and cadence.

# Drill: Numbers 0–99

| | | | |
|---|---|---|---|
| 54 | 15 | 80 | 63 |
| 78 | 24 | 8 | 89 |
| 96 | 49 | 92 | 50 |
| 99 | 82 | 53 | 44 |
| 35 | 87 | 36 | 81 |
| | | | |
| 88 | 83 | 1 | 41 |
| 59 | 2 | 67 | 62 |
| 6 | 79 | 16 | 69 |
| 55 | 10 | 70 | 21 |
| 64 | 97 | 7 | 72 |
| | | | |
| 11 | 75 | 73 | 27 |
| 18 | 76 | 26 | 68 |
| 77 | 23 | 25 | 61 |
| 22 | 57 | 14 | 20 |
| 71 | 60 | 5 | 19 |
| | | | |
| 66 | 29 | 56 | 12 |
| 17 | 52 | 9 | 84 |
| 90 | 33 | 38 | 98 |
| 51 | 47 | 45 | 48 |
| 91 | 86 | 37 | 85 |
| | | | |
| 94 | 43 | 3 | 32 |
| 42 | 0 | 46 | 39 |
| 58 | 74 | 28 | 13 |
| 30 | 65 | 4 | 93 |
| 95 | 31 | 34 | 40 |

# Things on the Tube

➤ **Suggested Activity:** Using the TV schedule provided below, answer the following questions:

1.  What channel will "Friends" be on this Saturday?

2.  What channel will "The Simpsons" be on this Sunday?

3.  What channel will "General Hospital" be on this Saturday?

4.  What channel will "Boston Public" be on this Sunday?

5.  What channel will "The Practice" be on this Sunday?

6.  What channel will "Frasier" be on this Saturday?

7.  What channel will "Ally McBeal" be on this Saturday?

8.  What channel will "Will & Grace" be on this Sunday?

9.  What channel will "ER" be on this Saturday?

10. What channel will "The Young and the Restless" be on this Sunday?

| SATURDAY | | |
|---|---|---|
| **Time** | **Channel** | **Program** |
| 11:00 a.m. | 4 | As The World Turns |
| 3:00 p.m. | 6 | General Hospital |
| 4:00 p.m. | 5 | Frasier |
| 6:30 p.m. | 8 | ER |
| 8:00 p.m. | 7 | Ally McBeal |
| 10:00 p.m. | 9 | Friends |
| **SUNDAY** | | |
| **Time** | **Channel** | **Program** |
| 10:00 a.m. | 9 | The Young and the Restless |
| 1:30 p.m. | 3 | Guiding Light |
| 2:00 p.m. | 4 | The Simpsons |
| 2:30 p.m. | 6 | Boston Public |
| 5:00 p.m. | 2 | Will & Grace |
| 7:30 p.m. | 5 | The Practice |

# Around the Room

➤ **Suggested Activity:** In a group, have the first person sign 1, the second person sign 2, etc., up to 100. Then repeat the activity, going backwards; the first person signs 100, the second person signs 99, etc.

# 100 on the Dot

➤ **Suggested Activity:** Arrange seats in a circle. Decide who will go first. That student chooses a number between 1 and 10, and signs it. The next student chooses a number between 1 and 10 and adds to the first student's number, signing the sum. This continues around the circle, with each person signing the new sum, until one person can add a number that makes 100 . . . on the dot.

# ▶ Unit Two: Hundreds

- ❖ **Warm-Up Exercises**

- ❖ **Overview**

- ❖ **Drills: Hundreds**
  **More Hundreds**
  **Hundreds Incorporating Teens and Twenties**

- ❖ **Activities: Dewey Decimal Game**
  **Let's Get Personal**

# Warm-Up Exercises

**Shoulder Shrugs:** Slowly raise and drop shoulders several times.

**The Swan Dive:** Slowly stretch arms above your head until they meet, palms together. Gently lower them to shoulder level, palms up. Repeat.

**Finger Lifts:** Place hand palm down on a table or flat surface and slowly raise and lower each finger. Repeat with the other hand.

**Full Arm Stretch:** Hold arm out parallel to the floor, palm down. Lock elbow. Raise your hand so the fingertips point to the ceiling. With the other hand, gently press the raised fingers back toward your body for a five-count. Alternate with the other hand. Repeat twice.

**Palm Press:** Press palms together in front of your body. Keeping your elbows high, use the right palm to gently and slowly push the left palm backwards, from the wrist only, toward the left elbow. Slowly and gently, use the left palm to push the right palm backwards, from the wrist only, toward the right elbow. Repeat several times.

**The Frankenstein:** With arms stretched out in front of you, palms down, slowly open and close hands, stretching the fingers apart as far as possible. Repeat several times.

**Wrist Revolutions:** With closed hands, slowly rotate wrists in toward each other several times. Then rotate wrists away from each other several times.

## Overview

### Hundreds

The formal sign for 100, 200, 300, . . . 900, is 1 + C, 2 + C, 3 + C, . . . 9 + C.

A typical variant for 100–500 is created by forming a representation of the "C" with only the number sign involved. Therefore, 400 would be made by signing 4 and then crooking/bending those four fingers, still separated, and pulling back slightly.

**400**

Note: This variant can be used as a stand-alone for 200–500, but not for 100. 100 is signed 1 + C, but once additional numbers are incorporated (e.g., 101, 156, 188), the variant can be employed. This variant can only be used for 100–500; the numbers 600–900 must be signed 6 + C, 7 + C, 8 + C, and 9 + C.

# Drill: Hundreds

| | | | |
|---|---|---|---|
| 642 | 369 | 825 | 901 |
| 753 | 470 | 936 | 112 |
| 147 | 223 | 975 | 692 |
| 258 | 334 | 186 | 703 |
| 362 | 445 | 297 | 814 |
| | | | |
| 470 | 556 | 308 | 925 |
| 581 | 667 | 419 | 136 |
| 692 | 778 | 521 | 247 |
| 713 | 889 | 632 | 358 |
| 864 | 581 | 824 | 991 |
| | | | |
| 743 | 469 | 935 | 112 |
| 398 | 915 | 580 | 667 |
| 844 | 561 | 145 | 212 |
| 388 | 951 | 589 | 656 |
| 176 | 793 | 368 | 445 |
| | | | |
| 409 | 126 | 691 | 778 |
| 166 | 783 | 367 | 434 |
| 854 | 571 | 146 | 222 |
| 511 | 237 | 712 | 889 |
| 612 | 348 | 822 | 989 |
| | | | |
| 955 | 672 | 256 | 323 |
| 287 | 804 | 479 | 556 |
| 733 | 459 | 934 | 101 |
| 277 | 894 | 478 | 545 |
| 501 | 237 | 711 | 878 |
| | | | |
| 622 | 348 | 823 | 990 |
| 499 | 126 | 690 | 767 |
| 965 | 682 | 247 | 334 |
| 279 | 422 | 858 | 640 |
| 225 | 123 | 169 | 459 |
| | | | |
| 323 | 592 | 812 | 947 |
| 460 | 325 | 876 | 423 |
| 561 | 477 | 835 | 793 |
| 723 | 935 | 317 | 167 |
| 851 | 512 | 137 | 682 |

# Drill: More Hundreds

| | | | |
|---|---|---|---|
| 527 | 671 | 148 | 160 |
| 849 | 915 | 460 | 782 |
| 383 | 271 | 804 | 494 |
| 848 | 961 | 459 | 582 |
| 627 | 738 | 248 | 359 |
| | | | |
| 283 | 382 | 704 | 893 |
| 850 | 272 | 471 | 793 |
| 161 | 472 | 682 | 950 |
| 515 | 959 | 126 | 405 |
| 493 | 737 | 904 | 348 |
| | | | |
| 394 | 504 | 815 | 516 |
| 638 | 259 | 749 | 172 |
| 360 | 926 | 693 | 115 |
| 137 | 212 | 577 | 994 |
| 454 | 225 | 836 | 318 |
| | | | |
| 421 | 167 | 991 | 624 |
| 381 | 535 | 232 | 723 |
| 341 | 248 | 174 | 825 |
| 491 | 223 | 823 | 270 |
| 623 | 281 | 375 | 541 |
| | | | |
| 592 | 693 | 911 | 625 |
| 157 | 227 | 587 | 615 |
| 320 | 158 | 392 | 268 |
| 627 | 348 | 237 | 153 |
| 298 | 125 | 804 | 425 |
| | | | |
| 726 | 310 | 575 | 999 |
| 699 | 755 | 133 | 722 |
| 866 | 244 | 843 | 466 |
| 155 | 299 | 577 | 933 |
| 688 | 322 | 344 | 677 |
| | | | |
| 366 | 533 | 899 | 855 |
| 744 | 888 | 488 | 922 |
| 977 | 799 | 566 | 444 |
| 522 | 166 | 877 | 433 |
| 355 | 788 | 933 | 766 |

# Drill: Hundreds Incorporating Teens and Twenties

| | | | |
|---|---|---|---|
| 215 | 321 | 419 | 528 |
| 618 | 727 | 316 | 422 |
| 520 | 629 | 719 | 828 |
| 417 | 523 | 621 | 711 |
| 820 | 929 | 518 | 624 |
| | | | |
| 722 | 812 | 921 | 111 |
| 619 | 725 | 823 | 913 |
| 122 | 212 | 720 | 826 |
| 924 | 114 | 223 | 313 |
| 821 | 927 | 125 | 215 |
| | | | |
| 324 | 414 | 922 | 128 |
| 226 | 316 | 425 | 515 |
| 123 | 229 | 327 | 417 |
| 526 | 616 | 224 | 320 |
| 428 | 518 | 627 | 717 |
| | | | |
| 325 | 421 | 529 | 619 |
| 728 | 818 | 426 | 522 |
| 611 | 720 | 829 | 919 |
| 527 | 623 | 712 | 821 |
| 911 | 120 | 628 | 724 |
| | | | |
| 813 | 922 | 112 | 221 |
| 729 | 825 | 914 | 123 |
| 213 | 322 | 811 | 926 |
| 115 | 224 | 314 | 423 |
| 912 | 127 | 216 | 325 |
| | | | |
| 415 | 524 | 113 | 228 |
| 317 | 426 | 516 | 625 |
| 214 | 329 | 418 | 527 |
| 617 | 726 | 315 | 411 |
| 519 | 628 | 718 | 827 |
| | | | |
| 416 | 512 | 620 | 729 |
| 819 | 928 | 517 | 613 |
| 721 | 811 | 920 | 129 |
| 618 | 714 | 822 | 912 |
| 121 | 211 | 719 | 815 |

# Dewey Decimal Game

➤ **Suggested Activity:** Divide into pairs. Each student takes a different list of Dewey Decimal System numbers for a variety of topics. Ask and answer the following questions using the tables below.

1.  What do I consider when buying a camera?

2.  Where can I find a Farmer's Almanac?

3.  I need a book about Michelangelo.

4.  Where can I find a copy of the Chicago Tribune?

5.  How do you keep score in baseball?

6.  I need a copy of Outdoor Life.

7.  Where can I find an Italian dictionary?

8.  Are there any books about The Beatles?

9.  Where can I find a book about the famous architect Frank Lloyd Wright?

10. Where can I find books about the Protestant Reformation?

## Dewey Decimal System

| 000 | COMPUTERS, INTERNET & SYSTEMS | 400 | LANGUAGE |
|---|---|---|---|
| 010 | Bibliographies | 410 | Linguistics |
| 020 | Library & information science | 420 | English & Old English languages |
| 030 | Encyclopedias & books of facts | 430 | German & related languages |
| 040 | [Unassigned] | 440 | French & related languages |
| 050 | Magazines, journals, and serials | 450 | Italian, Romanian & related languages |
| 060 | Associations, organizations, & museums | 460 | Spanish & Portuguese languages |
| 070 | Journalism, publishing & news media | 470 | Latin & Italic languages |
| 080 | Quotations | 480 | Classical & modern Greek languages |
| 090 | Manuscripts and rare books | 490 | Other Languages |

# Dewey Decimal System—cont'd

| 200 | RELIGION | 700 | ARTS |
|---|---|---|---|
| 210 | Philosophy & theory of religion | 710 | Landscaping & area planning |
| 220 | The Bible | 720 | Architecture |
| 230 | Christianity & Christian theology | 730 | Sculpture, ceramics, & metalworks |
| 240 | Christian practice and observance | 740 | Drawing & decorative arts |
| 250 | Christian pastoral practice and religious orders | 750 | Painting |
| 260 | Church organization, social work & worship | 760 | Graphic arts |
| 270 | History of Christianity | 770 | Photography |
| 280 | Christian denominations | 780 | Music |
| 290 | Other religions | 790 | Sports, games & entertainment |

# Let's Get Personal

➤ **Suggested Activity:** With a partner, share the following numerical information (real or invented). Be sure to use appropriate ASL structure and grammatical features.

1. Me:
   - Age?
   - Birthdate?
   - Social security number?
   - Phone number?

2. My Family:
   - Parents' ages?
   - Siblings' ages?
   - Number of pets?
   - Number of children?

3. Food:
   - Number of times you eat out per week?
   - Slices of pizza usually consumed in one sitting?
   - Number of canned/bottled carbonated beverages you drink per week?
   - Daily calorie intake?

4. Intimate Details:
   - How many times per day do you brush your teeth?
   - How many bottles of cologne or perfume do you have?
   - How many pairs of shoes do you own?
   - How many pictures of family and friends do you have in your wallet?

# Unit Three: Thousands, Millions, and Billions

- ❖ **Warm-Up Exercises**

- ❖ **Overview**

- ❖ **Drills:** **Thousands**
  **Tens of Thousands**
  **Hundreds of Thousands, Millions, and Billions**

- ❖ **Activities:** **Points of Light Shelter Statistics**
  **Population of the World's Largest Cities**
  **The Greatest Show on Earth**
  **Telephone Game**

# Warm-Up Exercises

**Shoulder Shrugs:** Slowly raise and drop shoulders several times.

**The Swan Dive:** Slowly stretch arms above your head until they meet, palms together. Gently lower them to shoulder level, palms up. Repeat.

**Finger Lifts:** Place hand palm down on a table or flat surface and slowly raise and lower each finger. Repeat with the other hand.

**Full Arm Stretch:** Hold arm out parallel to the floor, palm down. Lock elbow. Raise your hand so the fingertips point to the ceiling. With the other hand, gently press the raised fingers back toward your body for a five-count. Alternate with the other hand. Repeat twice.

**Palm Press:** Press palms together in front of your body. Keeping your elbows high, use the right palm to gently and slowly push the left palm backwards, from the wrist only, toward the left elbow. Slowly and gently, use the left palm to push the right palm backwards, from the wrist only, toward the right elbow. Repeat several times.

**The Frankenstein:** With arms stretched out in front of you, palms down, slowly open and close hands, stretching the fingers apart as far as possible. Repeat several times.

**Wrist Revolutions:** With closed hands, slowly rotate wrists in toward each other several times. Then rotate wrists away from each other several times.

# Overview

### Thousands

THOUSAND is signed:

When the numbers 1–5 are in the "thousands" position, the palm faces out. For example, in the numbers 2,879 and 4,690, the 2 and the 4 will face out.

Numbers above 999 should be signed reflecting their decimal placements and grouping; 321,615 would be signed as THREE-HUNDRED TWENTY-ONE THOUSAND SIX-HUNDRED FIFTEEN.

Additionally, although a number like 1,500 may be spoken as "fifteen hundred," ASL would generally convert it to ONE THOUSAND FIVE HUNDRED.

## Millions

MILLION is signed

**1,000,000**

## Billions and Trillions

The words "billion" and "trillion" are fingerspelled.

# Drill: Thousands

| | | | |
|---|---|---|---|
| 1,655 | 8,322 | 2,744 | 5,077 |
| 4,966 | 9,411 | 3,877 | 4,988 |
| 3,855 | 1,633 | 9,433 | 8,300 |
| 2,866 | 3,611 | 6,344 | 1,499 |
| 6,188 | 5,099 | 4,722 | 2,500 |
| | | | |
| 5,833 | 7,111 | 8,566 | 9,277 |
| 1,244 | 9,099 | 3,255 | 5,611 |
| 3,488 | 9,144 | 7,622 | 8,233 |
| 2,366 | 4,388 | 6,477 | 4,688 |
| 6,533 | 1,777 | 1,066 | 5,599 |
| | | | |
| 4,522 | 7,355 | 2,199 | 2,844 |
| 3,766 | 6,733 | 8,977 | 7,855 |
| 7,518 | 1,317 | 4,816 | 5,655 |
| 8,015 | 4,911 | 2,222 | 7,032 |
| 5,917 | 2,207 | 1,829 | 2,540 |
| | | | |
| 3,506 | 1,123 | 6,319 | 3,316 |
| 7,510 | 4,031 | 1,321 | 2,184 |
| 1,700 | 3,636 | 1,972 | 8,119 |
| 6,363 | 9,461 | 1,050 | 7,639 |
| 2,211 | 4,414 | 8,123 | 3,431 |
| | | | |
| 2,690 | 1,741 | 7,207 | 5,539 |
| 6,496 | 4,273 | 8,585 | 2,716 |
| 8,251 | 3,359 | 6,044 | 4,228 |
| 4,298 | 2,965 | 8,579 | 4,042 |
| 7,311 | 6,202 | 1,854 | 5,309 |
| | | | |
| 2,864 | 9,531 | 5,113 | 3,076 |
| 6,410 | 3,935 | 1,642 | 7,480 |
| 9,743 | 4,187 | 8,426 | 3,864 |
| 4,975 | 2,753 | 1,757 | 9,668 |
| 6,399 | 7,521 | 5,298 | 8,632 |
| | | | |
| 3,016 | 9,405 | 4,278 | 8,823 |
| 5,430 | 7,611 | 6,651 | 6,430 |
| 7,893 | 5,258 | 8,025 | 1,489 |
| 1,789 | 6,239 | 9,101 | 6,066 |
| 4,834 | 3,906 | 1,238 | 1,568 |

# Drill: Tens of Thousands

| | | | |
|---|---|---|---|
| 20,315 | 12,168 | 48,711 | 62,397 |
| 63,336 | 45,505 | 97,725 | 25,416 |
| 25,173 | 90,628 | 67,531 | 64,208 |
| 36,284 | 89,517 | 78,642 | 53,197 |
| 12,840 | 76,420 | 13,951 | 47,395 |
| | | | |
| 90,864 | 79,515 | 32,086 | 66,420 |
| 81,739 | 22,608 | 45,173 | 80,628 |
| 44,208 | 35,173 | 92,840 | 33,719 |
| 70,628 | 56,284 | 31,975 | 68,406 |
| 44,714 | 22,936 | 55,825 | 71,322 |
| | | | |
| 77,047 | 69,433 | 44,592 | 66,933 |
| 88,158 | 55,603 | 58,544 | 44,377 |
| 22,545 | 61,477 | 66,989 | 88,111 |
| 27,733 | 99,434 | 77,090 | 12,822 |
| 99,211 | 66,101 | 97,888 | 55,665 |
| | | | |
| 77,212 | 44,554 | 55,807 | 23,466 |
| 33,481 | 28,955 | 99,269 | 52,599 |
| 11,222 | 17,233 | 46,577 | 22,370 |
| 37,055 | 88,323 | 33,656 | 97,844 |
| 22,322 | 33,066 | 18,399 | 44,913 |
| | | | |
| 14,677 | 23,799 | 33,433 | 70,277 |
| 11,579 | 24,062 | 91,739 | 65,319 |
| 69,517 | 87,531 | 23,951 | 46,284 |
| 88,642 | 42,017 | 20,810 | 77,531 |
| 34,711 | 58,406 | 10,844 | 42,218 |
| | | | |
| 70,835 | 11,946 | 91,153 | 45,389 |
| 75,380 | 34,279 | 90,264 | 55,719 |
| 56,498 | 39,724 | 92,057 | 20,835 |
| 81,946 | 78,486 | 48,613 | 66,491 |
| 12,057 | 64,820 | 23,168 | 57,502 |

# Drill: Hundreds of Thousands, Millions, and Billions

| | | | |
|---|---|---|---|
| 137,508 | 916,886 | 785,873 | 446,439 |
| 572,942 | 349,139 | 118,166 | 992,985 |
| 896,984 | 452,520 | 683,153 | 248,619 |
| 335,328 | 113,494 | 557,549 | 127,997 |
| 359,720 | 238,308 | 563,651 | 794,664 |
| | | | |
| 779,767 | 907,095 | 461,831 | 828,522 |
| 805,913 | 674,762 | 229,217 | 668,658 |
| 392,036 | 727,713 | 148,411 | 660,489 |
| 426,253 | 901,955 | 843,581 | 365,669 |
| 993,126 | 359,580 | 935,692 | 484,147 |
| | | | |
| 515,174 | 328,873 | 819,834 | 576,258 |
| 282,247 | 704,095 | 296,752 | 337,332 |
| 668,369 | 474,748 | 852,510 | 692,976 |
| 175,631 | 583,827 | 751,470 | 471,368 |
| 965,391 | 629,357 | 398,024 | 510,246 |
| | | | |
| 1,641,423 | 4,092,138 | 6,528,630 | 2,475,397 |
| 3,359,569 | 5,142,940 | 9,237,681 | 7,348,754 |
| 8,300,875 | 1,658,638 | 2,775,107 | 9,492,982 |
| 5,944,406 | 1,506,215 | 3,142,203 | 2,035,837 |
| 8,378,431 | 9,962,527 | 4,531,632 | 9,885,607 |
| | | | |
| 65,324,467 | 40,579,021 | 22,911,688 | 93,849,770 |
| 10,439,895 | 23,103,684 | 44,208,765 | 30,161,633 |
| 90,454,975 | 14,894,722 | 26,021,668 | 88,233,864 |
| 42,783,277 | 78,931,854 | 40,767,111 | 92,677,313 |
| 54,303,855 | 64,305,115 | 38,946,399 | 76,119,427 |
| | | | |
| 136,046,935,815 | 258,281,629,803 | 7,470,425,069 | 27,357,045,839 |
| 9,273,361,769 | 26,338,414,957 | 5,182,597,148 | 47,286,037,136 |
| 119,259,583,991 | 48,247,181,626 | 94,036,171,471 | 8,162,148,703 |
| 70,051,583,969 | 4,624,712,259 | 12,823,555,477 | 13,657,412,883 |

# Points of Light Shelter Statistics

➤ **Suggested Activity:** With a partner, ask and answer the questions below using the table provided.

1. How many people were served in April 1998? November 1999?

2. Monthly average of people served in 1998?

3. Total number of people served in 2001?

4. Lowest number of people served in 1999?

5. Highest number of people served in 2000?

6. How many people were served in October 1998?

7. Monthly average of people served in 1999?

8. How many people were served in August 1998? August 1999? August 2000? August 2001?

9. Total number of people served in 2000?

10. How many people were served in May 2001?

## Total People Served

|           | 1998   | 1999   | 2000   | 2001   |
|-----------|--------|--------|--------|--------|
| January   | 4,238  | 4,781  | 6,070  | 6,622  |
| February  | 5,010  | 4,185  | 5,205  | 6,359  |
| March     | 3,997  | 4,606  | 6,176  | 7,049  |
| April     | 4,269  | 3,869  | 5,265  | 5,686  |
| May       | 3,908  | 3,785  | 5,096  | 5,533  |
| June      | 3,690  | 3,784  | 4,387  | 5,587  |
| July      | 4,706  | 3,338  | 3,320  | 4,286  |
| August    | 4,706  | 3,402  | 3,528  | 4,514  |
| September | 4,330  | 3,890  | 4,293  | 5,019  |
| October   | 5,047  | 4,028  | 5,245  | 6,092  |
| November  | 5,081  | 3,969  | 5,546  | 6,353  |
| December  | 5,494  | 4,194  | 5,548  | 5,563  |
| Total     | 54,476 | 47,831 | 59,679 | 69,027 |
| Monthly Avg. | 4,540 | 3,986 | 4,973 | 5,752 |

# Population of the World's Largest Cities

➤ **Suggested Activity:** Chose a city and sign the population to a partner, who then identifies the city.

## Projected Populations for 2015

| | |
|---|---|
| Tokyo, Japan | 28,887,659 |
| Mexico City, Mexico | 19,180,723 |
| Sao Paulo, Brazil | 20,320,481 |
| New York City, US | 17,602,326 |
| Bombay, India | 26,218,015 |
| Shanghai, China | 17,969,167 |
| Los Angeles, US | 14,218,246 |
| Calcutta, India | 17,305,592 |
| Buenos Aires, Argentina | 13,856,834 |
| Seoul, South Korea | 12,980,908 |
| Beijing, China | 15,570,622 |
| Osaka, Japan | 10,609,000 |
| Lagos, Nigeria | 24,640,010 |
| Rio de Janeiro, Brazil | 11,860,751 |
| Delhi, India | 16,860,473 |

# The Greatest Show on Earth

➤ **Suggested Activity:** Using the following circus trivia, ask and answer the questions below with a partner:

1.   How many horses does the circus own?

2.   How many pounds of carrots are consumed each year?

3.   How many countries does the circus go to?

4.   How much does the train weigh fully loaded?

5.   How many lions, tigers, and bears does the circus have altogether?

6.   How many hours does it take to set up for a performance?

7.   How many different costumes do they have?

8.   How many people see the circus each year?

9.   How many performances are given each year?

10.   How many loaves of bread do the animals eat in a year?

---

**Circus Trivia**

Entertains 25 million people in 97 countries each year

Gives 1,075 performances each year

Uses more than 1,000 costumes

Takes about 8 hours to set up before a performance

Animals:      42 elephants
              10 lions
              14 tigers
              6 bears
              33 horses
              2 camels
              2 llamas
              4 zebras

Each year the animals eat:      364 tons of hay
                                46,800 pounds of meat
                                62,400 pounds of carrots
                                39,000 pounds of apples
                                15,288 loaves of bread

Circus train: has 53 cars; the fully loaded train weighs 1.5 billion pounds

# Telephone Game

➤ **Suggested Activity:** Divide into equal groups and form lines. The first person in each line faces the instructor, the rest turn around. The instructor signs one of the following numbers including the context prompt one time only to the front row of students. They then turn and tap the next person in line, and sign the same number with context, one time only. The process continues through the line until the last person has seen the number. That person comes to the front of the line and signs it back to the instructor. Teams with the correct number score one point.

October 1998

$1,282

Year 1967

119,259,583,991

7,869 horses

Year 1863

17,712 people

12,823,555,477

May 2001

5,555 elephants

Total 69,027

$33,209

93,849,770

533 cars

August 1999

Year 1776

8,022 lions

27,357,045,839

Total 54,476

Year 1994

# Unit Four: Telephone Numbers, Addresses, Zip Codes, and Social Security Numbers

❖ **Warm-Up Exercises**

❖ **Overview**

❖ **Drills:  Telephone Numbers**
**Zip Codes**

❖ **Activities:  Business Cards**
**How Far?**
**Dewey Decimal Game**
**Number Relay**

# Warm-Up Exercises

**Shoulder Shrugs:** Slowly raise and drop shoulders several times.

**The Swan Dive:** Slowly stretch arms above your head until they meet, palms together. Gently lower them to shoulder level, palms up. Repeat.

**Finger Lifts:** Place hand palm down on a table or flat surface and slowly raise and lower each finger. Repeat with the other hand.

**Full Arm Stretch:** Hold arm out parallel to the floor, palm down. Lock elbow. Raise your hand so the fingertips point to the ceiling. With the other hand, gently press the raised fingers back toward your body for a five-count. Alternate with the other hand. Repeat twice.

**Palm Press:** Press palms together in front of your body. Keeping your elbows high, use the right palm to gently and slowly push the left palm backwards, from the wrist only, toward the left elbow. Slowly and gently, use the left palm to push the right palm backwards, from the wrist only, toward the right elbow. Repeat several times.

**The Frankenstein:** With arms stretched out in front of you, palms down, slowly open and close hands, stretching the fingers apart as far as possible. Repeat several times.

**Wrist Revolutions:** With closed hands, slowly rotate wrists in toward each other several times. Then rotate wrists away from each other several times.

# Overview

### Telephone Numbers

Telephone numbers can be signed in a variety of ways by incorporating natural groupings or easily remembered number pairings. Note the variations for the telephone number 365-4639 in the following examples:

3-6-5-4-6-3-9              3-6-5-46-39              3-65-46-39

### Addresses

Addresses can be also grouped/paired. Note the variations in the following examples:

| | | |
|---|---|---|
| 3-26 Sycamore Dr. | 6-8-7-5 Elm Ave. | 1-4-2-8-4 Oak St. |
| 3-2-6 Sycamore Dr. | 68-75 Elm Ave. | 14-2-84 Oak St. |
| | | 1-42-84 Oak St. |

### Zip Codes

Zip codes follow the same patterns:

9-2-4-3-1
9-24-31

### Social Security Numbers

Social Security numbers also follow the same patterns:

2-4-0 (pause) 3-4 (pause) 9-7-1-6
2-4-0 (pause) 3-4 (pause) 97-16
2-40-34-97-16

# Drill: Telephone Numbers

| | | |
|---|---|---|
| 243-5809 | 770-4201 | 333-6644 |
| 734-1844 | 338-7200 | 562-5485 |
| 277-7851 | 727-8961 | 353-2001 |
| 264-0218 | 688-3550 | 258-0581 |
| | | |
| 827-4449 | 586-6945 | 463-3005 |
| 495-6559 | 248-7880 | 235-7743 |
| 745-7715 | 786-1319 | 533-5191 |
| 274-7296 | 871-6489 | 750-0750 |
| | | |
| 562-4913 | 589-3797 | 722-1909 |
| 345-9905 | 885-4899 | 907-3456 |
| 522-5200 | 474-7055 | 542-1207 |
| 333-6620 | 887-1186 | 495-1447 |
| | | |
| 349-9343 | 586-1820 | 694-2254 |
| 349-6023 | 478-1701 | 586-8164 |
| 892-8714 | 588-5018 | 321-2271 |
| 561-2454 | 272-4904 | 566-0777 |
| | | |
| 561-2488 | 279-1300 | 625-5268 |
| 376-4000 | 690-4850 | 522-2217 |
| 887-7575 | 563-0909 | 955-8770 |
| 694-4338 | 239-1888 | 352-0135 |
| | | |
| 272-9193 | 266-9911 | 435-2445 |
| 454-9800 | 891-1441 | 333-8102 |
| 276-8917 | 822-3780 | 265-1710 |
| 257-5220 | 762-0851 | 791-2759 |
| | | |
| 277-0045 | 952-2391 | 245-0126 |
| 562-2010 | 251-0701 | 688-9897 |
| 345-0707 | 538-8239 | 533-4487 |
| 999-9951 | 789-2181 | 587-4169 |
| | | |
| 783-1122 | 277-2511 | 522-1379 |
| 293-3014 | 262-9281 | 698-3612 |
| 338-6626 | 345-8778 | 463-3005 |
| 337-6086 | 847-0930 | 903-0762 |
| | | |
| 338-1122 | 955-7607 | 274-8523 |
| 337-7316 | 735-2964 | 651-5744 |
| 248-4552 | 542-8719 | 782-6090 |

# Drill: Zip Codes

| | | |
|---|---|---|
| 99508 | 99801 | 48864 |
| 84405 | 84107 | 21144 |
| 27709 | 80401 | 97211 |
| 48912 | 33308 | 33612 |
| 94539 | 60974 | 20707 |
| | | |
| 20002 | 98122 | 60077 |
| 94577 | 20902 | 48821 |
| 90713 | 90808 | 98116 |
| 20771 | 30602 | 45662 |
| 90006 | 55102 | 74128 |
| | | |
| 03301 | 33480 | 97361 |
| 48813 | 46204 | 33308 |
| 61531 | 33733 | 20850 |
| 14623 | 85718 | 20910 |
| 43123 | 48312 | 53190 |
| | | |
| 32561 | 60435 | 48066 |
| 06053 | 27233 | 40391 |
| 46350 | 85635 | 55330 |
| 87109 | 45855 | 34748 |
| 21222 | 97710 | 02886 |
| | | |
| 82604 | 28153 | 58767 |
| 14414 | 87018 | 38632 |
| 68104 | 59771 | 40214 |
| 66110 | 46540 | 06040 |
| 80219 | 77207 | 35807 |
| | | |
| 58501 | 03244 | 87113 |
| 53222 | 25064 | 98112 |
| 57103 | 76707 | 37397 |
| 12203 | 11767 | 49009 |
| 60089 | 95616 | 38305 |
| | | |
| 28621 | 10011 | 08852 |
| 55104 | 66106 | 40291 |
| 04813 | 99567 | 39821 |
| 21109 | 87694 | 53877 |
| 64970 | 72316 | 82169 |

# Business Cards

➤ **Suggested Activity:** Using the following "business cards" practice signing addresses, including zip codes and telephone numbers. (Collect real business cards for additional practice.)

| | |
|---|---|
| **UNIVERSAL CLEANING, INC.**<br>Chester Shonkwiler, Manager<br>12895 Oneida Woods Trail<br>Pewamo, VA 59867<br>(272) 982-5196 | **Real Estate Associates**<br>Sabrina Polihonki<br>496 Plum Tree Circle<br>Silver Springs, MD 20910<br>(298) 806-5329 |
| **Daniel L. Esmay**<br>Attorney at Law<br>2978 Binghamton Drive<br>Jacksonville, FL 68253<br>(321) 641-8152 | **General Motors, Operations**<br>Marcus A. Swartz<br>TPC West 660 South Blvd<br>Raleigh, NC 39521<br>(364) 249-8573 |
| **Statewide Services for the Deaf**<br>Michael Douglas, CI & CT<br>202 E. Kalamazoo Drive, #200-A<br>Gaylord, MO 43951<br>(876) 634-8767<br>www.mdouglasshi.org | **Fine Jewelry**<br>Carl Greve, CEO<br>317 S. W. Morrison Street<br>Portland, OR 50279<br>(800) 284-4420<br>egreve@carlgreve.com |
| **THE WOODEN SKATE**<br>Olivia Hayden-Meyers, Owner<br>4524 Wild Blossom Lane<br>Springfield, IL 36481<br>(482) 346-7524 | **Rochelle Jackson, CI & CT**<br>Nationally Certified Interpreter<br>635 Hubbard Hill Lane<br>Albany, NY 99957<br>(663) 524-0122 Voice/TTY |
| **HICKS STUDIO**<br>16927 Sycamore Street<br>Baltimore, Maryland 21207<br>(410) 658-2369 | **FAMILY DENTISTRY**<br>Patricia Jury-Cranson, D.D.S.<br>3606 Nature Bounty Way<br>Sheridan, LA 69586<br>(589) 472-3614 |
| **THE MAC**<br>*RANDALL JOSEPH EMERY, ASSOCIATE*<br>*3708 SPIKE LANE*<br>*HUDSON, TN 64827*<br>*(461) 893-4695* | **O'BRIEN AGENCY, INC.**<br>Tony O'Brien, Sr., CEO<br>7200 N. Colby Lake Road<br>Laingsburg, MA 82591<br>(225) 347-6914 |

# How Far?

➤ **Suggested Activity:** With a partner, take turns answering the questions below, incorporating the appropriate ASL signs for cities and states.

1. How far is it between St. Louis and Detroit?

2. How far is it between Atlanta and Washington D.C.?

3. How far is it between Phoenix and Boston?

4. How far is it between New Orleans and San Francisco?

5. How far is it between Buffalo and Los Angeles?

6. How far is it between San Francisco and Atlanta?

7. How far is it between Los Angeles and Phoenix?

8. How far is it between Detroit and New Orleans?

9. How far is it between Boston and Buffalo?

10. How far is it between Washington D.C. and St. Louis?

| Distance in miles to/from | Atlanta, GA | Boston, MA | Buffalo, NY | Detroit, MI | Los Angeles, CA | New Orleans, LA | Phoenix, AZ | St. Louis, MO | San Francisco, CA | Washington, D.C. |
|---|---|---|---|---|---|---|---|---|---|---|
| Atlanta, GA | .... | 933 | 695 | 595 | 1935 | 427 | 1592 | 467 | 2133 | 542 |
| Boston, MA | 933 | .... | 398 | 613 | 2590 | 1359 | 2295 | 1036 | 2696 | 392 |
| Buffalo, NY | 695 | 398 | .... | 218 | 2195 | 1087 | 1904 | 662 | 2298 | 290 |
| Detroit, MI | 595 | 613 | 218 | .... | 1976 | 938 | 1685 | 452 | 2087 | 397 |
| Los Angeles, CA | 1935 | 2590 | 2195 | 1976 | .... | 1675 | 357 | 1585 | 345 | 2295 |
| New Orleans, LA | 427 | 1359 | 1087 | 938 | 1675 | .... | 1318 | 1433 | 1898 | 968 |
| Phoenix, AZ | 1592 | 2295 | 1904 | 1685 | 357 | 1318 | .... | 1270 | 652 | 1980 |
| St. Louis, MO | 467 | 1036 | 662 | 452 | 1585 | 1433 | 1270 | .... | 1738 | 710 |
| San Francisco, CA | 2133 | 2696 | 2298 | 2087 | 345 | 1898 | 652 | 1738 | .... | 2437 |
| Washington D.C. | 542 | 392 | 290 | 397 | 2295 | 968 | 1980 | 710 | 2437 | .... |

# Dewey Decimal Game

➤ **Suggested Activity:** Divide into pairs. Each student takes a different list of Dewey Decimal System numbers for a variety of topics. Ask and answer the following questions using the tables below.

1.  Where can I find information about the Electoral College?

2.  How about information on parrots?

3.  Where are the books on dinosaurs?

4.  Where can I find Miss Manners' books?

5.  Where would I find Walt Whitman's "Leaves of Grass"?

6.  I need a book of Grimms' Fairy Tales.

7.  Where can I find a book about volcanoes?

8.  How can I find out when the Americans with Disabilities Act was passed?

9.  Where can I find pictures of poison ivy?

10. I need information about the moons of Saturn.

## Dewey Decimal System

| 300 | SOCIAL SCIENCES, SOCIOLOGY & ANTHROPOLOGY | 800 | LITERATURE, RHETORIC & CRITICISM |
|---|---|---|---|
| 310 | Statistics | 810 | American literature in English |
| 320 | Political science | 820 | English & Old English literatures |
| 330 | Economics | 830 | German & related literatures |
| 340 | Law | 840 | French & related literatures |
| 350 | Public administration & military science | 850 | Italian, Romanian & related literatures |
| 360 | Social problems & social services | 860 | Spanish & Portuguese literatures |
| 370 | Education | 870 | Latin & Italic literatures |
| 380 | Commerce, communication & transportation | 880 | Classical & modern Greek literatures |
| 390 | Customs, etiquette & folklore | 890 | Other literatures |

## Dewey Decimal System—cont'd

| 500 | SCIENCE | | |
|---|---|---|---|
| 510 | Mathematics | | |
| 520 | Astronomy | | |
| 530 | Physics | | |
| 540 | Chemistry | | |
| 550 | Earth sciences & geology | | |
| 560 | Fossils & prehistoric life | | |
| 570 | Biology & life sciences | | |
| 580 | Plants (Botany) | | |
| 590 | Animals (Zoology) | | |

# Number Relay

➤ **Suggested Activity:** Divide into teams and form lines. The first person in each line goes to the blackboard, ready to write. The instructor picks a number from the list below and signs it. The first student to correctly write the number on the board wins a point for their team. Students then pass the chalk to the next student in line and go to the back of the line.

Social Security: 379-74-6567
Phone number: 352-4114
4,382,511 people
23 camels
666 tons of hay
12 hours a day
101 Dalmatians
Social Security: 289-11-8549
1,500 daily calories
Social Security: 357-69-3232
42,469 dollars per year
Phone number: 810-876-2141
808 pounds of carrots
$3,327
73 years old
Phone number: 287-9014
$100,000
11 sisters
Social Security number: 068-49-1835
50 states
29 llamas

# ▶ Unit Five: Time and Age

- ❖ **Warm-Up Exercises**

- ❖ **Overview**

- ❖ **Drill: Time**

- ❖ **Activities: Don't Miss the Bus!**
  **Numbers Are from Venus and Mars and . . .**
  **Day Planner**
  **Planner**

# Warm-Up Exercises

**Shoulder Shrugs:** Slowly raise and drop shoulders several times.

**The Swan Dive:** Slowly stretch arms above your head until they meet, palms together. Gently lower them to shoulder level, palms up. Repeat.

**Finger Lifts:** Place hand palm down on a table or flat surface and slowly raise and lower each finger. Repeat with the other hand.

**Full Arm Stretch:** Hold arm out parallel to the floor, palm down. Lock elbow. Raise your hand so the fingertips point to the ceiling. With the other hand, gently press the raised fingers back toward your body for a five-count. Alternate with the other hand. Repeat twice.

**Palm Press:** Press palms together in front of your body. Keeping your elbows high, use the right palm to gently and slowly push the left palm backwards, from the wrist only, toward the left elbow. Slowly and gently, use the left palm to push the right palm backwards, from the wrist only, toward the right elbow. Repeat several times.

**The Frankenstein:** With arms stretched out in front of you, palms down, slowly open and close hands, stretching the fingers apart as far as possible. Repeat several times.

**Wrist Revolutions:** With closed hands, slowly rotate wrists in toward each other several times. Then rotate wrists away from each other several times.

## Overview

### Time

Time is signed like digital clock time, with TIME incorporated in the message. "A quarter past 10" is signed TIME 10 + 15. "A quarter 'til 11:00" is signed TIME 10 + 45.

When signing "on the hour" (5:00, 3:00, 9:00), the number sign incorporates a small shake, unless the sign already has movement incorporated into it (10, 11, 12).

Two variants are used when signing "on the hour," one where the dominant hand index finger taps the passive wrist and then moves into the number sign, and one where the base of the palm/wrist of the dominant hand, which already incorporates the number sign, taps the passive wrist.

When signing 12 o'clock, the signs NOON or MIDNIGHT are used, or the variants NOON (with the incorporated sign 12) or MIDNIGHT (with the incorporated sign 12).

When signing a combination of hours and minutes (5:20, 3:55, 9:07), the hour sign does not shake.

To indicate am or pm use the sign morning, afternoon, or night before signing the time.

### Age

Signing age incorporates the sign OLD, as in OLD 7. Less formally, when indicating the ages 1–9 the OLD sign can be dropped and the number itself slides down from the chin. To indicate someone is seven years old, the sign SEVEN, with the index finger touching the chin, drops from the chin to the natural sign space.

To indicate the span of a decade, the "tens" number sign shakes:

**Example:** Tim is in his 30's

OLD 3 (shake)

**30s**

# Drill: Time

| | | | |
|---|---|---|---|
| 8:15 am | 3:05 am | 4:10 am | 8:00 am |
| 12:05 pm | 10:45 pm | 11:15 pm | 9:50 pm |
| 6:35 pm | 5:55 am | 10:35 pm | 5:15 am |
| 8:30 pm | 1:00 pm | 1:05 am | 6:00 pm |
| | | | |
| 6:45 am | 3:45 am | 10:15 pm | 11:20 pm |
| 12:15 am | 9:10 am | 2:25 am | 8:50 am |
| 7:15 pm | 4:00 pm | 8:45 pm | 9:00 pm |
| 2:15 am | 3:30 pm | 4:05 pm | 1:10 am |
| | | | |
| 7:00 pm | 4:55 am | 10:30 am | 5:10 am |
| 1:15 pm | 12:30 am | 2:30 am | 8:55 pm |
| 9:30 am | 10:25 pm | 11:35 pm | 3:10 am |
| 9:45 pm | 12:50 am | 6:25 am | 10:40 pm |
| | | | |
| 11:45 pm | 5:30 am | 5:50 pm | 11:40 pm |
| 1:30 am | 6:40 pm | 7:25 am | 12:55 am |
| 12:10 pm | 4:50 am | 6:30 pm | 2:00 am |
| 3:35 am | 9:15 am | 2:45 pm | 11:30 am |
| | | | |
| 4:45 pm | 11:25 am | 8:10 am | 2:20 pm |
| 9:55 pm | 3:15 pm | 3:40 am | 10:00 pm |
| 4:30 pm | 6:15 am | 10:20 pm | 11:00 am |
| 9:05 am | 7:20 pm | 5:45 am | 12:00 am |
| | | | |
| 12:45 pm | 8:05 am | 5:05 pm | 7:40 am |
| 7:30 am | 7:45 pm | 7:35 pm | 3:00 am |
| 5:00 am | 4:15 am | 6:20 am | 1:45 pm |
| 1:25 am | 5:40 pm | 2:10 am | 9:35 pm |
| | | | |
| 1:20 pm | 6:50 am | 12:40 pm | 9:25 am |
| 5:35 am | 10:10 pm | 11:55 am | 2:05 pm |
| 12:20 pm | 2:50 am | 6:25 pm | 11:10 am |
| 9:40 pm | 5:25 am | 6:05 am | 1:35 pm |
| | | | |
| 7:33 am | 11:50 pm | 9:20 pm | 4:25 pm |
| 2:35 pm | 10:03 pm | 7:50 am | 3:20 am |
| 7:05 am | 12:25 am | 4:35 pm | 1:40 pm |
| 3:50 pm | 5:20 am | 8:25pm | 6:10 pm |

**Suggested Extra Practice:** Include practicing the signs for early morning, morning, early afternoon, afternoon, night, and late night with these times.

# Don't Miss the Bus!

➤ **Suggested Activity:** Using the bus schedule provided, answer the questions below with a partner:

1.  On Tuesday, the bus leaves the Transit Center at 7:20 am. What time will it arrive at County Hospital?

2.  On Saturdays Grant Mall closes at 6:00 pm. If you want to spend at least an hour shopping, what time do you have to catch the bus at 18th & Oak?

3.  Your house is a 10-minute walk from 13th & Main and you have an appointment at the County Hospital at 10:45 in the morning. On a weekday, what time do you leave your house to arrive on time for the appointment?

4.  On a Saturday, what time would you leave to make the same appointment time?

5.  What time do you have to arrive at the Transit Center, if you want to see the 1:30 afternoon movie at the mall on Wednesday? on Saturday?

6.  Weekday visiting hours at County Hospital are 8:00 am to 11:15 am and again from 3:00 pm until 8:45 pm. If your apartment is at 13th & Main, what times can you catch a bus and be sure to arrive with time for an hour-and-a-half visit?

7.  What time does the last bus get to Grant Mall on a weekday?

8.  Approximately what time will you get to 18th & Oak, if you leave the Transit Center at 7:22 pm on a Saturday?

9.  What is the earliest time you can take the bus from the Transit Center on a weekday?

10. If I miss the 11:52 am bus from 13th & Main on a Saturday morning, when is the next bus scheduled to leave the same stop?

## Bus Schedule

| Transit Center | 13th & Main | 18th & Oak | County Hospital | Grant Mall |
|---|---|---|---|---|
| **Weekdays** | | | | |
| 7:20 | 7:27 | 7:34 | 7:43 | 7:57 |
| 9:10 | 9:17 | 9:24 | 9:33 | 9:43 |
| 11:05 | 11:12 | 11:19 | 11:28 | 11:38 |
| 1:00 | 1:07 | 1:14 | 1:23 | 1:37 |
| 3:00 | 3:08 | 3:15 | 3:27 | 3:40 |
| 4:40 | 4:48 | 4:55 | 5:07 | 5:20 |
| 6:15 | 6:22 | 6:28 | 6:37 | 6:47 |
| 8:25 | 8:32 | 8:38 | 8:47 | 8:57 |
| **Saturday** | | | | |
| 8:52 | 8:59 | 9:04 | 9:13 | 9:24 |
| 11:45 | 11:52 | 11:57 | 12:06 | 12:17 |
| 2:45 | 2:52 | 2:57 | 3:06 | 3:17 |
| 5:45 | 5:52 | 5:57 | 6:06 | 6:17 |
| 7:22 | 7:29 | 7:34 | 7:43 | 7:54 |

# Numbers Are from Venus, and Mars and...

➤ **Suggested Activity:** Using the following statistics, answer the questions below with a partner:

1.  Which planet has the largest diameter? What is that diameter?

2.  Which planet has the smallest diameter? What is that diameter?

3.  How long does it take for Mars to revolve around the sun?

4.  How long does it take for Pluto to make one full rotation on its own axis?

5.  How far is Neptune from the sun?

6.  Which planet takes the most time to revolve around the sun? How long does it take?

7.  Which planet takes the least time to revolve around the sun? How long does it take?

8.  Which planet is closest to the sun? What is its distance from the sun? How long does it take for it to make one full rotation on its own axis?

9.  Cite all the statistics listed here that are related to your favorite planet.

10. What is the period of revolution and the period of rotation for the 3rd planet out from the sun?

| Planet | Distance from Sun (miles) | Diameter (miles) | Period of Revolution | Period of Rotation |
|---|---|---|---|---|
| Mercury | 35,960,000 | 3,100 | 88 days | 57 days |
| Venus | 67,200,000 | 7,700 | 225 days | 247 days |
| Earth | 92,900,000 | 7,918 | 365.25 days | 23 hrs. 56 min. |
| Mars | 141,500,000 | 4,200 | 687 days | 24 hrs. 37 min. |
| Jupiter | 483,400,000 | 89,000 | 11.86 years | 9 hrs. 55 min. |
| Saturn | 886,200,000 | 71,500 | 29.5 years | 10 hrs. 14 min. |
| Uranus | 1,783,000,000 | 30,000 | 84 years | 10 hrs. 45 min. |
| Neptune | 2,790,000,000 | 27,700 | 164.75 years | 15 hrs. 45min. |
| Pluto | 3,670,000,000 | 3,664 | 248.5 years | 6.4 days |

# Day Planner

➤ **Suggested Activity A:** Divide into pairs. Using the activities below, or your own, fill in the planner on the next page with five activities, in the day and time you will do them. Sign your plans for the week to your partner, who records them on the planner. When finished, compare schedules to make sure they match.

➤ **Suggested Activity B:** In pairs, and using one schedule between you, plan a mutual schedule together, with 10 activities.

## Activities

Dinner at Olive Garden

Watch "Wheel of Fortune"

Rollerblading

Pedicure or manicure

Visit grandma

Go to the zoo

ASL class

Study group

Movie

Latte with mother

Water aerobics

Tae Kwan Do class

Couch potato time

Breakfast

Lunch

Dinner

Brunch

Grocery shopping

Laundry

Surfing the Web

Shopping for clothes

Waterskiing

# Planner

| MONDAY ___/___/___ Activity | TUESDAY ___/___/___ Activity | WEDNESDAY ___/___/___ Activity |
|---|---|---|
| 7:00<br>7:15<br>7:30<br>7:45 | 7:00<br>7:15<br>7:30<br>7:45 | 7:00<br>7:15<br>7:30<br>7:45 |
| 8:00<br>8:15<br>8:30<br>8:45 | 8:00<br>8:15<br>8:30<br>8:45 | 8:00<br>8:15<br>8:30<br>8:45 |
| 9:00<br>9:15<br>9:30<br>9:45 | 9:00<br>9:15<br>9:30<br>9:45 | 9:00<br>9:15<br>9:30<br>9:45 |
| 10:00<br>10:15<br>10:30<br>10:45 | 10:00<br>10:15<br>10:30<br>10:45 | 10:00<br>10:15<br>10:30<br>10:45 |
| 11:00<br>11:15<br>11:30<br>11:45 | 11:00<br>11:15<br>11:30<br>11:45 | 11:00<br>11:15<br>11:30<br>11:45 |
| 12:00<br>12:15<br>12:30<br>12:45 | 12:00<br>12:15<br>12:30<br>12:45 | 12:00<br>12:15<br>12:30<br>12:45 |
| 1:00<br>1:15<br>1:30<br>1:45 | 1:00<br>1:15<br>1:30<br>1:45 | 1:00<br>1:15<br>1:30<br>1:45 |
| 2:00<br>2:15<br>2:30<br>2:45 | 2:00<br>2:15<br>2:30<br>2:45 | 2:00<br>2:15<br>2:30<br>2:45 |
| 3:00<br>3:15<br>3:30<br>3:45 | 3:00<br>3:15<br>3:30<br>3:45 | 3:00<br>3:15<br>3:30<br>3:45 |
| 4:00<br>4:15<br>4:30<br>4:45 | 4:00<br>4:15<br>4:30<br>4:45 | 4:00<br>4:15<br>4:30<br>4:45 |
| 5:00<br>5:15<br>5:30<br>5:45 | 5:00<br>5:15<br>5:30<br>5:45 | 5:00<br>5:15<br>5:30<br>5:45 |
| 6:00<br>6:15<br>6:30<br>6:45 | 6:00<br>6:15<br>6:30<br>6:45 | 6:00<br>6:15<br>6:30<br>6:45 |
| 7:00<br>7:15<br>7:30<br>7:45 | 7:00<br>7:15<br>7:30<br>7:45 | 7:00<br>7:15<br>7:30<br>7:45 |
| 8:00<br>8:15<br>8:30<br>8:45 | 8:00<br>8:15<br>8:30<br>8:45 | 8:00<br>8:15<br>8:30<br>8:45 |

# Unit Six: Time Measurement

❖ **Warm-Up Exercises**

❖ **Overview**

❖ **Activities:** **How Long Does It Take?**
**Let's Get Personal**
**Getting Creative**
**Number Relay**

# Warm-Up Exercises

**Shoulder Shrugs:** Slowly raise and drop shoulders several times.

**The Swan Dive:** Slowly stretch arms above your head until they meet, palms together. Gently lower them to shoulder level, palms up. Repeat.

**Finger Lifts:** Place hand palm down on a table or flat surface and slowly raise and lower each finger. Repeat with the other hand.

**Full Arm Stretch:** Hold arm out parallel to the floor, palm down. Lock elbow. Raise your hand so the fingertips point to the ceiling. With the other hand, gently press the raised fingers back toward your body for a five-count. Alternate with the other hand. Repeat twice.

**Palm Press:** Press palms together in front of your body. Keeping your elbows high, use the right palm to gently and slowly push the left palm backwards, from the wrist only, toward the left elbow. Slowly and gently, use the left palm to push the right palm backwards, from the wrist only, toward the right elbow. Repeat several times.

**The Frankenstein:** With arms stretched out in front of you, palms down, slowly open and close hands, stretching the fingers apart as far as possible. Repeat several times.

**Wrist Revolutions:** With closed hands, slowly rotate wrists in toward each other several times. Then rotate wrists away from each other several times.

# Overview

## Time Measurement

The numbers 1–9 can be incorporated to form a compound sign with MINUTE, HOUR, DAY, WEEK and MONTH.

When incorporating numbers into WEEK (2-WEEK, 8-WEEK), the numbers 1–5 are formed with the knuckles/palm of the dominant hand sliding along the palm of the passive hand. When the numbers 6–9 are incorporated, for visual clarity the sign is raised, so the base of the palm/wrist slides along the upper palm of the passive hand.

When creating tense, there are some variations. For example, when signing PAST-WEEK and FUTURE-WEEK, the numbers 1–3 can be incorporated. However, the sign 4-WEEK-AGO is generally not signed, but converted to PAST-MONTH.

When incorporating numbers into MONTH (3-MONTH, 4-MONTH), the numbers 1–5 are formed with the back of the dominant hand, palm in, sliding down the passive base.

When the numbers 6–9 are incorporated (7-MONTH), this pattern may continue, or a variant may be used. The variant turns palm out, with the base of the palm/wrist sliding down the passive base.

The numbers 1–9 can be incorporated to form a compound sign with YEAR. However, the numbers 1–5 can be incorporated into the sign for NEXT-YEAR and PAST-YEAR.

# How Long Does It Take?

➤ **Suggested Activity:** Create an ASL sentence to share with the rest of the class, about the time it takes for something to happen, based on the information below.

**It takes. . .**

1. 4 seconds
   to say the McDonald's Big Mac tongue twister: "two all beef patties, special sauce, lettuce, cheese, pickles, onions, on a sesame seed bun."

2. 37 seconds
   to deal a deck of 52 cards.

3. 52 Seconds
   to reach the 86th floor observatory of the Empire State Building by elevator.

4. 1 minute
   for the average adult to read 300 words.

5. 2 minutes, 30 seconds
   to bake a potato in a microwave oven.

6. 3 minutes
   to steep tea.
   to cook a 3-minute egg.

7. 3 minutes, 30 seconds
   to milk a cow producing 10 pounds of milk daily.

8. 12 minutes
   for a bedbug to gorge itself on human blood.

9. 14 minutes
   to broil a 2-inch-thick filet mignon rare.

10. 15 minutes
    for a stripper to lose 36 calories during his or her act.

11. 20 minutes
    to boil lasagna noodles until tender.

12. 36 minutes
    to produce an Oscar Mayer wiener.

13. 48 minutes
    for the average American to commute to work.

# How Long Does It Take?—continued

14. 1 hour
    for Parker Brothers to print $392,000 in Monopoly money.
    for a B-58 bomber to travel 1,528 miles.

15. 1 hour 49 minutes
    to view the Hitchcock thriller "Psycho."

16. 1 hour 50 minutes
    for Bobby Fisher to win 19 games of chess in 1970.

17. 3 hours 40 minutes
    to view "Gone With the Wind."

18. 3 hours 59 minutes 51 seconds
    to listen to Marx Brothers radio program excerpts on an album entitled "3 hours,
    59 minutes, 51 seconds with the Marx Brothers."

19. 5 hours
    for food to be completely digested in the human stomach.

20. 5 hours 36 minutes
    for a frog embryo to grow 32 cells.

21. 6 hours 15 minutes
    to roast a 22-lb turkey.

22. 10 hours
    for a shearer to clip 200 sheep.

23. 12 hours
    for a caterer's staff of 280 to set tables for a dinner party for 4,000 people.

24. 15 hours
    for a 1- to 3-month-old infant to get his daily sleep requirement

25. 33 hours 29 minutes 30 seconds
    for Charles A. Lindbergh to fly solo from Minneola, New York nonstop to Paris in
    1927 in The Spirit of St. Louis.

26. 8 days
    for a pair of average-quality pantyhose to wear out, according to the "Consumers
    Report Buying Guide."

# Let's Get Personal

➤ **Suggested Activity:** With a partner, share the following numerical information (factual or invented). Be sure to use appropriate ASL structure and grammatical features.

1.  Sports Trivia:
    - Number of holes in golf?
    - Length of an Olympic sized pool?
    - Laps on a track to run a mile?
    - Length of a football field?

2.  Dream Vacation:
    - Seat number?
    - Hours by plane?
    - Time plane took off? Landed?
    - Length of stay?

3.  Home Sweet Home:
    - Total square footage?
    - Size of lot?
    - Size of master bedroom?
    - Number of closets?

# Getting Creative

➤ **Suggested Activity:** With a partner, create a story incorporating the following numeric information.

1. **High School Years:**
   Number of students in each grade
   Number of periods in the school day
   Number of male teachers you had
   Your locker combination

2. **College Life:**
   Years attended
   Total enrollment
   Credit hours taken
   Number of times you changed your major

3. **News Flash:**
   Date
   Time
   Number of rioters
   Hours spent at the hospital

4. **Directions:**
   Highway numbers
   Exit numbers
   House number
   Phone number

5. **Birthday Girl:**
   Date of birthday
   Number of candles
   Number of presents
   Number of people at the party

6. **Public Transportation:**
   Bus number
   Time it takes to get where you are going
   Number of transfers
   Time of day

# Number Relay

➤ **Suggested Activity:** Divide into teams and form lines. The first person in each line goes to the blackboard, ready to write. The instructor signs an item from the list below. The first student to correctly write the number on the board wins a point for his/her team. Students then pass the chalk to the next student in line and go to the back of the line.

$3,314

Year 1952

Phone number: (714) 425-0552

84,123 pineapples

$7,811

Year 1973

Phone number: (410) 269-7697

49,017 buttons

2,566 pencils

Year 1991

Phone number: (302) 284-8599

61,883 tangerines

Student number: 00185

6,728 flags

Year 1825

Phone number: (787) 870-3541

Student number: 34648

5,215 compact discs

$8,063

Year 1969

Phone number: (207) 561-4500

Student number: 55330

Phone number: (616) 927-7174

$5,940

Year 1721

# ► Unit Seven: Decades and Centuries

- ❖ **Warm-Up Exercises**

- ❖ **Overview**

- ❖ **Drill: Years**

- ❖ **Activities: They Lived, They Died**
  **100 Freestyle Olympic Champions**
  **School District Enrollment**
  **Average SAT Test Scores**

# Warm-Up Exercises

**Shoulder Shrugs:** Slowly raise and drop shoulders several times.

**The Swan Dive:** Slowly stretch arms above your head until they meet, palms together. Gently lower them to shoulder level, palms up. Repeat.

**Finger Lifts:** Place hand palm down on a table or flat surface and slowly raise and lower each finger. Repeat with the other hand.

**Full Arm Stretch:** Hold arm out parallel to the floor, palm down. Lock elbow. Raise your hand so the fingertips point to the ceiling. With the other hand, gently press the raised fingers back toward your body for a five-count. Alternate with the other hand. Repeat twice.

**Palm Press:** Press palms together in front of your body. Keeping your elbows high, use the right palm to gently and slowly push the left palm backwards, from the wrist only, toward the left elbow. Slowly and gently, use the left palm to push the right palm backwards, from the wrist only, toward the right elbow. Repeat several times.

**The Frankenstein:** With arms stretched out in front of you, palms down, slowly open and close hands, stretching the fingers apart as far as possible. Repeat several times.

**Wrist Revolutions:** With closed hands, slowly rotate wrists in toward each other several times. Then rotate wrists away from each other several times.

# Overview

### Decades

As when signing decade-related age information, the span of a decade is signed by shaking the "tens" number sign:

During the 1970s
HAPPEN 19 7(shake)

**1970s**

A handshape is sometimes used for "apostrophe S," where the ASL manual alphabet "S" twists from palm out to palm in. This variant would then be 19 70 + 'S (palm out to palm in).

### Centuries

A translation occurs when signing a specific century. For example, when discussing the 19th century, it is generally converted to its meaning of "the 1800s," and is signed 18 + C (and the C shakes). However, when talking specifically about the year 1800, sign 18-0-0.

The "apostrophe S," variant is also sometimes used for centuries. "The 1800s" would then be 18 C + 'S (palm out to palm in) or 1800 + 'S.

# Drill: Years

| | | | |
|---|---|---|---|
| 1983 | 1510 | 1911 | 1947 |
| 1504 | 1897 | 1929 | 1743 |
| 1936 | 1955 | 1853 | 1982 |
| 1805 | 1923 | 1960 | 1735 |
| | | | |
| 1916 | 1991 | 1609 | 1815 |
| 1854 | 1956 | 1949 | 1588 |
| 1922 | 1486 | 1995 | 1927 |
| 1967 | 1812 | 1895 | 1761 |
| | | | |
| 1924 | 1850 | 1948 | 1907 |
| 1970 | 1963 | 1875 | 1952 |
| 1720 | 1526 | 1925 | 1940 |
| 1040 | 1713 | 2005 | 1225 |
| | | | |
| 1992 | 1972 | 2036 | 1946 |
| 1981 | 1608 | 1592 | 1959 |
| 1842 | 1980 | 1808 | 1906 |
| 1976 | 1988 | 1723 | 1632 |
| | | | |
| 2000 | 1873 | 1738 | 1619 |
| 1759 | 1933 | 1765 | 1928 |
| 1926 | 1454 | 1444 | 1864 |
| 1971 | 1987 | 1921 | 2002 |
| | | | |
| 1999 | 1990 | 1868 | 1958 |
| 1827 | 1910 | 1311 | 1939 |
| 1931 | 1937 | 1403 | 1776 |
| 1829 | 1961 | 2010 | 1658 |
| | | | |
| 1646 | 1622 | 1978 | 1408 |
| 1957 | 1517 | 1965 | 1974 |
| 1920 | 1901 | 1966 | 1834 |
| 1862 | 1913 | 1945 | 1798 |
| | | | |
| 1884 | 1930 | 1602 | 1741 |
| 1950 | 1989 | 1580 | 1893 |
| 1980 | 1977 | 1703 | 1851 |
| 1994 | 1918 | 1696 | 1786 |
| 1400s | 1800s | 1700s | 1900s |
| the 17th Century | the 20th Century | the 16th Century | the 7th Century |

# They Lived, They Died

➤ **Suggested Activity:** In groups of three, one student fingerspells a name, another signs when that person was born, and a third signs when the person died.

| Name | Born | Died |
|------|------|------|
| William Shakespeare | 1564 | 1616 |
| Erma Bombeck | 1927 | 1996 |
| Hannibal | 247 B.C. | 183 B.C. |
| Mary Shelley | 1797 | 1851 |
| Red Skelton | 1913 | 1997 |
| Edgar Allan Poe | 1809 | 1849 |
| Martin Luther King, Jr. | 1929 | 1968 |
| Kurt Cobain | 1967 | 1994 |
| Tilly Edinger | 1897 | 1967 |
| Indira Gandhi | 1917 | 1984 |
| Akira Kurosawa | 1910 | 1998 |
| Henry VIII | 1491 | 1547 |
| Florence Griffith Joyner | 1959 | 1998 |
| Davy Crockett | 1786 | 1836 |
| Princess Diana | 1961 | 1997 |
| Julius Caesar | 100 B.C. | 44 B.C. |
| Lou Fant | 1932 | 2001 |
| Isadora Duncan | 1878 | 1927 |
| Orville Redenbacher | 1907 | 1995 |
| John Milton | 1608 | 1674 |
| James Herriot | 1916 | 1995 |
| Beatrix Potter | 1866 | 1943 |
| Dante | 1265 | 1321 |
| Richard Farnsworth | 1920 | 2000 |
| Geronimo | 1829 | 1909 |
| Gianlorenzo Bernini | 1598 | 1680 |
| Tupac Shakur | 1971 | 1996 |
| Joan of Arc | 1414 | 1431 |
| Joe DiMaggio | 1914 | 1999 |
| Louis Armstrong | 1900 | 1971 |
| Jim Henson | 1936 | 1990 |
| Lydia Liliuokalani | 1838 | 1917 |
| Marie Phillip | 1953 | 1997 |
| Malcolm X | 1925 | 1965 |
| Juliette Gordon Low | 1860 | 1927 |
| Gene Rodenberry | 1921 | 1991 |
| Charles Schulz | 1922 | 2000 |
| Deng Xiaopeng | 1904 | 1997 |
| Margaret Hamilton | 1902 | 1985 |
| Vincent Price | 1911 | 1993 |
| Laura Redden Searing | 1840 | 1923 |

# 100 Freestyle Olympic Champions

➤ **Suggested Activity:** In groups of three, one student signs a year, the next student spells the name of the swimmer, and the third student signs the corresponding Olympic time.

| Year | Swimmer | Olympic Time (minutes/seconds) |
|---|---|---|
| 1896 | Alfred Hajos, Hungary | 1:22.20 |
| 1904 | Zolton de Halmay, Hungary | 1:02.80 |
| 1908 | Charles Daniel, US | 1:05.60 |
| 1912 | Duke Kahanmoku, US | 1:03.40 |
| 1920 | Duke Kahanmoku, US | 1:01.40 |
| 1924 | Johnny Weismuller, US | 59.00 |
| 1928 | Johnny Weismuller, US | 58.60 |
| 1932 | Yasuji Miyazaki, Japan | 58.20 |
| 1936 | Ferenc Csik, Hungary | 57.60 |
| 1948 | Wally Ris, US | 57.30 |
| 1952 | Clark Scholes, US | 57.40 |
| 1956 | Jon Henricks, Australia | 55.40 |
| 1960 | John Devitt, Australia | 55.20 |
| 1964 | Don Schollander, US | 53.40 |
| 1968 | Mike Wenden, Australia | 52.20 |
| 1972 | Mark Spitz, US | 51.20 |
| 1976 | Jim Montgomery, US | 49.99 |
| 1980 | Jog Worthe, E. Germany | 50.40 |
| 1984 | Rowdy Gaines, US | 49.80 |
| 1988 | Matt Biondi, US | 48.63 |
| 1992 | Aleksandr Popov, Unified team | 49.02 |
| 1996 | Aleksandr Popov, Russia | 48.74 |
| 2000 | Peter Vanden Hoogenband, Denmark | 47.84 |

# School District Enrollment

➤ **Suggested Activity:** With a partner, take turns asking and answering the following questions using the chart provided:

1. How many elementary students were enrolled in 1995?

2. How many secondary students were enrolled in 1987?

3. How many students were receiving special services in 2000?

4. What was the total number of students enrolled in 1981?

5. How many students were receiving special services in 1989?

6. How many elementary students were enrolled in 1998?

7. How many secondary students were enrolled in 1983?

8. What was the total number of students enrolled in 1990?

9. How many students were receiving special services in 1986?

10. How many elementary students were enrolled in 1980?

# School District Enrollment, 1980–2000

| Year | No. of Elementary Students | No. of Secondary Students | No. of Special Services Students | Total No. of Students |
|------|------|------|------|------|
| 1980 | 21,763 | 15,398 | 187 | 37,348 |
| 1981 | 22,433 | 16,402 | 237 | 39,072 |
| 1982 | 22,450 | 17,151 | 238 | 39,839 |
| 1983 | 21,510 | 17,341 | 322 | 39,173 |
| 1984 | 21,232 | 17,800 | 373 | 39,405 |
| 1985 | 21,634 | 18,093 | 414 | 40,141 |
| 1986 | 21,461 | 18,250 | 431 | 39,606 |
| 1987 | 21,283 | 17,887 | 436 | 39,606 |
| 1988 | 21,058 | 17,429 | 409 | 38,896 |
| 1989 | 20,596 | 16,360 | 376 | 36,908 |
| 1990 | 20,232 | 16,190 | 396 | 36,737 |
| 1991 | 20,596 | 17,378 | 361 | 37,357 |
| 1992 | 21,472 | 17,378 | 441 | 39,291 |
| 1993 | 21,971 | 17,832 | 624 | 40,427 |
| 1994 | 23,092 | 18,341 | 630 | 42,063 |
| 1995 | 23,440 | 18,237 | 749 | 42,426 |
| 1996 | 23,834 | 17,609 | 554 | 41,997 |
| 1997 | 23,511 | 16,890 | 506 | 40,907 |
| 1998 | 23,618 | 16,117 | 585 | 40,320 |
| 1999 | 23,943 | 16,311 | 565 | 40,819 |
| 2000 | 25,046 | 16,665 | 511 | 42,222 |

# Average SAT Test Scores

➤ **Suggested Activity:** Using the statistics provided, answer the questions below with a partner. Use appropriate ASL signs or fingerspelling for the states.

1. What were the 1980 and 1990 verbal scores for Indiana?

2. When Delaware's verbal score was 431, what was its math score?

3. What year did New Jersey students score 418 in the verbal portion?

4. What was the 1980 total for Vermont?

5. When students in Hawaii scored 481 in the math portion, what was their score in the verbal portion?

6. The year Florida had a total score of 888, what was Oregon's total score?

7. For the students in Texas, which score was higher: the 1990 total or the 1980 math?

8. What year did Maine score 463 in the math portion?

9. When Rhode Island scored 422 in the verbal portion, what was Vermont's math score?

10. When California's total was 903, what was Virginia's total?

## Statewide SAT Scores

| State | 1980 | | | 1990 | | |
|---|---|---|---|---|---|---|
| | Verbal | Math | Total | Verbal | Math | Total |
| California | 424 | 472 | 896 | 419 | 484 | 903 |
| Delaware | 431 | 469 | 900 | 433 | 470 | 903 |
| Florida | 424 | 464 | 888 | 418 | 466 | 884 |
| Georgia | 389 | 425 | 814 | 401 | 443 | 844 |
| Hawaii | 396 | 472 | 868 | 404 | 481 | 885 |
| Indiana | 407 | 450 | 857 | 408 | 459 | 867 |
| Maine | 427 | 467 | 894 | 423 | 463 | 886 |
| Maryland | 422 | 463 | 885 | 430 | 478 | 908 |
| New Jersey | 415 | 452 | 867 | 418 | 473 | 891 |
| Oregon | 427 | 465 | 892 | 439 | 484 | 923 |
| Rhode Island | 417 | 458 | 875 | 422 | 461 | 883 |
| Texas | 416 | 455 | 871 | 413 | 461 | 874 |
| Vermont | 432 | 468 | 900 | 431 | 466 | 897 |
| Virginia | 423 | 460 | 883 | 425 | 470 | 895 |

# Unit Eight: Money and Percents

- ❖ **Warm-Up Exercises**

- ❖ **Overview**

- ❖ **Activities: Here's a Tip**
  - **Home Prices in the USA**
  - **Let's Buy a House**
  - **Meal-Lodging Cost Index**
  - **Getting Creative**
  - **Let's Make a Car Deal**
  - **Vegetarian Restaurant**
  - **Shopping Trends**
  - **Do the Math**

# Warm-Up Exercises

**Shoulder Shrugs:** Slowly raise and drop shoulders several times.

**The Swan Dive:** Slowly stretch arms above your head until they meet, palms together. Gently lower them to shoulder level, palms up. Repeat.

**Finger Lifts:** Place hand palm down on a table or flat surface and slowly raise and lower each finger. Repeat with the other hand.

**Full Arm Stretch:** Hold arm out parallel to the floor, palm down. Lock elbow. Raise your hand so the fingertips point to the ceiling. With the other hand, gently press the raised fingers back toward your body for a five-count. Alternate with the other hand. Repeat twice.

**Palm Press:** Press palms together in front of your body. Keeping your elbows high, use the right palm to gently and slowly push the left palm backwards, from the wrist only, toward the left elbow. Slowly and gently, use the left palm to push the right palm backwards, from the wrist only, toward the right elbow. Repeat several times.

**The Frankenstein:** With arms stretched out in front of you, palms down, slowly open and close hands, stretching the fingers apart as far as possible. Repeat several times.

**Wrist Revolutions:** With closed hands, slowly rotate wrists in toward each other several times. Then rotate wrists away from each other several times.

# Overview

### Money

When signing dollar amounts, sign the number, then sign DOLLAR. A standard variant is used for 1–9 dollars, which twists the number sign from palm out to palm in. However, when signing 10 dollars and up, sign the number, then sign DOLLAR.

"Cents" values are signed by touching the forehead with the index finger (palm in). CENT may be signed before or after the number (e.g., a "quarter" can be signed as either CENT 25 or 25 CENT).

When signing 1–9 dollars with cents, as in $4.75, twist the 4 palm-out to palm-in, then return to palm-out for the 75 cents. "Cents" is implied, and is thus not signed.

There are a number of approaches used when signing dollar and cent combinations above 9 dollars. For example, $63.28 may be signed:

> 63 DOLLAR 28 CENT
>
> 63 DOLLAR 28

The decimal point in ASL is signed using the handshape of a boxed X, and is included in the following approach:

DOLLAR 63 DECIMAL-POINT 28

### Percents

Percents are signed as follows: the number is signed, palm out, followed by sign for PERCENT.

# Here's a Tip

➤ **Suggested Activity:** Choose a dollar amount. In pairs, one person calculates the total bill with a 15% tip, and one with a 20 % tip. For example, a check amount of $18.00 with a 15% tip is $20.70, and $21.60 with a 20% tip. ($18.00 + $2.70; $18.00 + $3.60)

| Check Amount | 15% | 20% |
| --- | --- | --- |
| $1.00 | $0.15 | $0.20 |
| $3.00 | $0.45 | $0.60 |
| $5.00 | $0.75 | $1.00 |
| $7.00 | $1.05 | $1.40 |
| $9.00 | $1.35 | $1.80 |
| $11.00 | $1.65 | $2.20 |
| $12.00 | $1.80 | $2.40 |
| $13.00 | $1.95 | $2.60 |
| $14.00 | $2.10 | $2.80 |
| $15.00 | $2.25 | $3.00 |
| $16.00 | $2.40 | $3.20 |
| $17.00 | $2.55 | $3.40 |
| $18.00 | $2.70 | $3.60 |
| $19.00 | $2.85 | $3.80 |
| $20.00 | $3.00 | $4.00 |
| $21.00 | $3.15 | $4.20 |
| $22.00 | $3.30 | $4.40 |
| $23.00 | $3.45 | $4.60 |
| $24.00 | $3.60 | $4.80 |
| $25.00 | $3.75 | $5.00 |
| $26.00 | $3.90 | $5.20 |
| $27.00 | $4.05 | $5.40 |
| $28.00 | $4.20 | $5.60 |
| $29.00 | $4.35 | $5.80 |
| $30.00 | $4.50 | $6.00 |
| $37.00 | $5.55 | $7.40 |
| $42.00 | $6.30 | $8.40 |
| $49.00 | $7.35 | $9.80 |
| $55.00 | $8.25 | $11.00 |
| $61.00 | $9.15 | $12.20 |
| $63.00 | $9.45 | $12.60 |
| $69.00 | $10.35 | $13.80 |
| $70.00 | $10.50 | $14.00 |
| $74.00 | $11.10 | $14.80 |
| $82.00 | $12.30 | $16.40 |
| $86.00 | $12.90 | $17.20 |
| $90.00 | $13.50 | $18.00 |
| $95.00 | $14.25 | $19.00 |
| $100.00 | $15.00 | $20.00 |

# Home Prices in the USA

➤ **Suggested Activity:** With a partner, one person signs/fingerspells a location, and the other responds with the corresponding price of a home there. Use the appropriate ASL sign or fingerspelling for the states.

## 1999 Home Prices for US Cities

Home = 2,200 square feet, 4-bedrooms, 2½ baths, family room, and double-car garage. Located in an area desirable for mid-level executive.

| City | Price | City | Price |
|------|-------|------|-------|
| Montgomery, AL | $107,215 | Omaha, NE | $108,635 |
| Juneau, AK | $133,330 | Reno, NV | $131,444 |
| Tucson, AZ | $128,533 | Nashua, NH | $210,777 |
| Little Rock, AR | $109,750 | Hunterdon, NJ | $243,250 |
| Beverly Hills, CA | $916,667 | Albuquerque, NM | $140,750 |
| Denver, CO | $108,167 | Rochester, NY | $150,000 |
| Danbury, CT | $257,665 | Raleigh, NC | $177,300 |
| Dover, DE | $128,500 | Fargo, ND | $153,400 |
| Tallahassee, FL | $124,000 | Toledo, OH | $124,000 |
| Savannah, GA | $107,750 | Tulsa, OK | $116,800 |
| Honolulu, HI | $438,333 | Portland, OR | $116,296 |
| Boise, ID | $82,677 | Harrisburg, PA | $158,881 |
| Bloomington, IL | $114,634 | Providence, RI | $223,669 |
| South Bend, IN | $91,600 | Charleston, SC | $128,150 |
| Des Moines, IA | $126,688 | Rapid City, SD | $118,025 |
| Topeka, KS | $130,583 | Nashville, TN | $129,188 |
| Louisville, KY | $123,667 | Arlington, TX | $98,332 |
| Shreveport, LA | $121,225 | Salt Lake City, UT | $125,500 |
| Bangor, ME | $167,230 | Burlington, VT | $218,143 |
| Baltimore, MD | $189,333 | Richmond, VA | $124,844 |
| Worchester, MA | $206,867 | Seattle, WA | $180,833 |
| East Lansing, MI | $147,783 | Charleston, WV | $131,667 |
| St. Paul, MN | $143,466 | Milwaukee, WI | $170,900 |
| Jackson, MS | $102,470 | Cheyenne, WY | $110,000 |
| Kansas City, MO | $119,975 | Vancouver, Canada | $288,257 |
| Great Falls, MT | $125,833 | | |

# Let's Buy a House

➤ **Suggested Activity:** One partner is a real estate agent who is trying to match a potential buyer with the right home from the listings below. Ask questions about the buyer's requirements for a house using input from the ads below, and select three ads that might meet them.

## Home Listings

Almost 1 Acre!
4 BR, 2.5 BA, double garage
$248,000

Up On Top
Great Views of the mountains!
2,296 SqFt PLUS
16,542 SqFt lot and horse property
$197,000

Assumable Mortgage
3 BR, 2.5 BA
Close to schools
$158,900

Fixer Upper Duplex
Ranch Style 1 BR, 1 BA
4-star energy rating
$89,000

Neptune Lake Condo
2 BR, 1 BA, storage
$59,000

LOG HOME!
16" Alaska Spruce Logs
3–4 BR, modeled after a lodge
built in the 1920's! Features 3 river-
rock fireplaces.
$785,000

Hidden Hills Exclusive
3 BR, 2.5 BA, 3-car garage
7,000 SqFt backs up to 10-acre
greenbelt. Built in '93
$299,000

Must Sell Now!
3 BR, 2.5 BA, 2,264 SqFt
2 decks, Jacuzzi
$214,000

Great Starter
2 BR, 1.5 BA townhouse
Perfect for first time buyer
$120,000

VA Approved Townhouse
2 BR, 3 BA, carport, small courtyard
Association Dues $210/month

Midtown Construction
5 minutes from downtown!
2,900 SqFt homes on wooded lots
Open house Sunday 1–4

Possible B & B
8 BR, 4 BA
9' ceilings, 3-car garage
4,803 SqFt, built in 1998
$449,900

Move in Now!
3 BR, 2 BA, next to park
Seller pays $2,000 in closing costs!
$156,175

Single Family Homes
1,609–2,400 SqFt
4 Floor plans to choose from!
$187,000–$214,5000

# Meal-Lodging Cost Index

➤ **Suggested Activity:** With a partner, and using the information in the table below, take turns asking and answering the following questions. Use appropriate ASL signs or fingerspelling for the states.

1. What is the range of rates for a single bed in Honolulu, HI?

2. Compare the low and high price for a room at the single corporate rate in Washington, DC.

3. Which city has the most expensive single bed rate?

4. Which city has the cheapest single bed rate?

5. For the 2 cities that have the lowest corporate rate, compare their high corporate rates.

6. If your company allows you to spend $41.00 a day for meals, where can you do business without having to spend extra on food?

7. Compare the low and high single corporate rates in Anchorage with those in San Francisco.

8. If you have $100 a day to spend for meals and lodging combined, which city would you go to and which type of lodging would you choose?

9. Compare the single low and high rates to the double low and high rates for Chicago.

10. Among those cities listed, which would you choose for a vacation? What type of lodging would you choose? Estimate your total expenses for meals and lodging for three days.

## Meals and Lodging Costs in Major U.S. Cities
## Peak Season 1999

| City, State | Single | | Single Corporate | | Double | | 3-Meal Total |
|---|---|---|---|---|---|---|---|
| | Low | High | Low | High | Low | High | |
| Anchorage, AK | $100 | $148 | $80 | $106 | $108 | $162 | $36 |
| Atlanta, GA | $95 | $146 | $88 | $137 | $106 | $166 | $40 |
| Boston, MA | $127 | $175 | $110 | $156 | $142 | $195 | $43 |
| Chicago, IL | $134 | $182 | $120 | $163 | $154 | $202 | $43 |
| Dallas, TX | $80 | $127 | $73 | $114 | $93 | $156 | $36 |
| Honolulu, HI | $139 | $202 | $119 | $178 | $141 | $202 | $45 |
| Las Vegas, NV | $63 | $96 | $54 | $85 | $63 | $97 | $44 |
| Manhattan, NY | $180 | $239 | $167 | $223 | $197 | $268 | $68 |
| New Orleans, LA | $66 | $111 | $54 | $88 | $69 | $117 | $37 |
| Philadelphia, PA | $98 | $144 | $84 | $125 | $107 | $160 | $39 |
| San Francisco, CA | $116 | $160 | $102 | $142 | $131 | $177 | $43 |
| Washington, D.C. | $138 | $185 | $116 | $161 | $156 | $211 | $46 |

# Getting Creative

➤ **Suggested Activity:** With a partner, create a story incorporating the following numeric information for each topic. Be prepared to share one of your stories in front of your class.

1.  Vacation:
    - Date of trip
    - Amount spent on souvenirs
    - Number of suitcases
    - Total cost of trip

2.  Grocery Shopping:
    - Store hours
    - Number of registers open
    - Total spent
    - Shopping time

3.  Real Estate:
    - Number of bedrooms
    - Number of bathrooms
    - Asking price
    - Purchasing price

4.  Personal Ad:
    - Height
    - Weight range
    - Age range
    - Years of education

5.  Lottery:
    - Winning numbers
    - Amount before taxes
    - Amount after taxes
    - Number of tickets purchased per year

# Let's Make a Car Deal

➤ **Suggested Activity:** Each student in the class is assigned one of the ads below. One student starts by "calling" one of the phone numbers and arranging to look at the car. The "seller" meets with the "buyer" and tries to sell his or her vehicle.

## Classified Ads—Cars and Trucks for Sale

| | |
|---|---|
| '83 Ford Ranger XL<br>5 speed<br>$1,950<br>694-4338 | '91 Toyota Landcruiser<br>117,000 miles<br>$14,700<br>239-1888 |
| '95 Grand Cherokee<br>V6, 88,000 miles<br>$6,400<br>522-2379 | '85 BMW<br>2 dr., 2 sets of tires<br>$2,700<br>387-8734 |
| '91 Jeep 4x4<br>1.0L, 4 dr, 98,000 miles<br>$5,700<br>783-7722 | '88 Chevy Cavalier<br>4 dr, tags 11/02<br>$1,500<br>564-9193 |
| '98 GMC SLE<br>½ ton extension cab<br>30 K miles, $22,600<br>277-2511 | '69 VW Beetle<br>2K+ miles<br>$450<br>698-3612 |
| '01 Suburban 1500<br>36 K mi, 9" tv /vcr<br>$32,750<br>892-8714 | '70 Ford Mustang Hatchback<br>1 owner<br>$1,800 Firm<br>522-2217 |
| '80 Toyota Tercel<br>2 dr., 5 speed, 35 mpg<br>$395<br>248-7880 | '92 Geo Prism<br>5 speed, 75K miles<br>$3,750<br>321-2271 |
| 2000 Z-71 Extended cab<br>3rd door, 5.3 L<br>$24,500 obo<br>786-1319 | '55 Chevy<br>½ ton Stepside<br>$11,000<br>495-1300 |
| '94 Nissan Sentra<br>Was asking $4,200<br>NOW $3,350<br>891-1441 | '99 Jeep Wrangler Sport<br>6 cyl., 34K miles<br>$14,500<br>566-0777 |

# Vegetarian Restaurant

➤ **Suggested Activity:** Divide into groups of three. Two students act as restaurant patrons, the third as their server. The patrons order from the menu below. The server writes down the ordered items, and then must calculate the final bill for the patrons. The patrons then calculate their total, including a tip.

---

## MENU

APPETIZERS

| | |
|---|---|
| Fresh Hand Rolled Tamales | $5.99 |
| Guacamole | $4.99 |
| Nachos Grande | $6.99 |
| Chile Con Questa | $3.99 |

COMBOS

| | |
|---|---|
| Veggie Burrito | $8.99 |
| Veggie Tacos | $7.99 |
| Veggie Enchilada | $9.99 |
| Veggie Chimichanga | $10.99 |
| Veggie Tamale | $6.99 |
| Veggie Flauta | $5.99 |

SIDES

| | |
|---|---|
| Flour Tortillas | $1.75 |
| Salsa | $2.99 |
| Guacamole | $4.25 |
| Sweet Corn Tomalito | $2.50 |
| Mexican Rice | $1.50 |
| Black Beans | $2.75 |
| Chips and Salsa | $3.99 |

BEVERAGES

| | |
|---|---|
| Herbal Tea | $2.00 |
| Fruit Juice | $1.75 |
| Natural Tea | $1.50 |
| Perrier | $1.25 |
| Milk | $1.10 |

# Shopping Trends

➤ **Suggested Activity:** Using the information in the survey below, partners take turns answering the questions below:

1. What percentage of those surveyed shopped at Nordstrom in 2000?

2. What percentage shopped at Fred Meyer in 1996?

3. What percentage shopped at Pricesavers in 1999?

4. What percentage shopped at Costco in 1997?

5. What percentage shopped at Longs in 1998?

6. What percentage shopped at Pay 'N Pak in 1999?

7. What percentage shopped at Sears in 2000?

8. What percentage shopped at Lamonts in 1997?

9. What percentage shopped at JC Penney in 1999?

10. What percentage shopped at Pay 'N Save in 1996?

## Shopping Survey Results
(Participant responses to the survey question:
Which of these stores have you shopped at in the
past 30 days, whether or not you bought anything?)

| Store | 1996 | 1997 | 1998 | 1999 | 2000 |
|-------|------|------|------|------|------|
| Costco | 35% | 36% | 34% | 32% | 42% |
| Fred Meyer | 60% | 61% | 67% | 66% | 71% |
| JC Penney | 36% | 32% | 38% | 31% | 35% |
| Lamonts | 45% | 46% | 50% | 45% | 47% |
| Longs | 42% | 37% | 30% | 34% | 33% |
| Nordstrom | 37% | 40% | 32% | 39% | 31% |
| Pay 'N Save | 80% | 73% | 72% | 71% | 68% |
| Pay 'N Pak | 29% | 25% | 26% | 20% | 21% |
| Pricesavers | 28% | 31% | 44% | 45% | 51% |
| Sears | 60% | 52% | 56% | 48% | 48% |

# Do the Math

➤ **Suggested Activity A:** The instructor signs the following math problems without the answer. Students respond with the correct answer.

➤ **Suggested Activity B:** The instructor writes the following problems on index/flash cards, and distributes them to students. In pairs, they must sign their problem to their partner, who must write the problem down in the form in which it was signed and compute the answer, and sign the answer back to their partner.

| | | |
|---|---|---|
| $10 \times 10 = 100$ | $15 \div 5 = 3$ | $42 - 9 = 31$ |
| $53 + 14 = 67$ | $300 + 800 = 1,100$ | $62 + 72 = 134$ |
| $100 - 75 = 25$ | $59 + 95 = 154$ | $5 \times 5 = 25$ |
| $396 \times 2 = 792$ | $11 \div 11 = 1$ | $298 - 98 = 200$ |
| $78 + 3 = 81$ | $604 - 24 = 580$ | $70 + 80 = 150$ |
| $13 + 23 = 36$ | $23 + 76 = 99$ | $53 - 33 = 20$ |
| $19 - 6 = 13$ | $50 \div 2 = 25$ | $26,015 \times 0 = 0$ |
| $12 \times 12 = 144$ | $9,876 - 876 = 9,000$ | $(7 \times 7) - 4 = 45$ |
| $99 \div 9 = 11$ | $246 + 357 = 603$ | $1 + 2 + 3 + 4 + 5 = 15$ |
| $178 + 3 = 181$ | $650 + 640 = 1,290$ | $1 \times 2 \times 3 \times 4 \times 5 = 120$ |

# Unit Nine: Pronouns, Height, and Measurement

- ❖ **Warm-Up Exercises**

- ❖ **Overview**

- ❖ **Activities:** **All about Animals**
  **Big and Small**
  **Let's Get Personal**
  **Hot, Cold, Rain, Snow**
  **Favorite Recipes**
  **Calorie and Fat Content**
  **Women's Basketball**

# Warm-Up Exercises

**Shoulder Shrugs:** Slowly raise and drop shoulders several times.

**The Swan Dive:** Slowly stretch arms above your head until they meet, palms together. Gently lower them to shoulder level, palms up. Repeat.

**Finger Lifts:** Place hand palm down on a table or flat surface and slowly raise and lower each finger. Repeat with the other hand.

**Full Arm Stretch:** Hold arm out parallel to the floor, palm down. Lock elbow. Raise your hand so the fingertips point to the ceiling. With the other hand, gently press the raised fingers back toward your body for a five-count. Alternate with the other hand. Repeat twice.

**Palm Press:** Press palms together in front of your body. Keeping your elbows high, use the right palm to gently and slowly push the left palm backwards, from the wrist only, toward the left elbow. Slowly and gently, use the left palm to push the right palm backwards, from the wrist only, toward the right elbow. Repeat several times.

**The Frankenstein:** With arms stretched out in front of you, palms down, slowly open and close hands, stretching the fingers apart as far as possible. Repeat several times.

**Wrist Revolutions:** With closed hands, slowly rotate wrists in toward each other several times. Then rotate wrists away from each other several times.

# Overview

### Pronouns

Pronoun incorporation uses both palm orientation and movement to indicate which people are being discussed.

The signs for 2-OF-US, 2-OF-YOU, and 2-OF-THEM use a slight back-and-forth shake between the identified parties. For 2-OF-US, the palm faces in, close to the shoulder, while for 2-OF-YOU and 2-OF-THEM, the palm faces up, shaking between referents.

In the incorporations 3-OF-US, 4-OF-US, etc., the palm orientation is also up, but the movement is a tight counter-clockwise circle for right-handed signers. Left-handed signers make a tight clockwise circle.

### Height

Height is described in feet and inches. To sign this, start with the "feet" measurement number, palm in, by the head. Then move the hand out, away from the head, while signing the "inches" measurement number. This context eliminates the need to add signs for feet and inches.

When the person being described is taller than the signer, the signer makes a slight upward movement for the "inches," also palm in. When the person is shorter, the signer makes a slight downward movement, palm in. When the person is approximately the same height, the movement is side-to-side, palm in.

### Measurement

Units of measurement are often fingerspelled abbreviations (ft, mm, tsp, lb, oz, mph). "Inches" is typically fingerspelled in contexts other than height, or represented by the sign MEASURE. "Degrees" can be fingerspelled, or represented by the sign TEMPERATURE.

Context is important when applying units of measurement: when talking about a pound of butter, "lb" is appropriate; when talking about a newborn 7-pound 3-ounce baby, the sign WEIGH is used: 7 POUND 3 O-Z.

# All about Animals

➤ **Suggested Activity:** With a partner, pick an animal and sign animal facts back and forth.

## Animal Facts

| Name | Height/Length | Weight | Other Facts |
|---|---|---|---|
| Grey Wolf | 25–32 inches (at shoulder) | 175 lbs. | A wolf's howl can be heard as far as 6 miles away. There are 4–7 cubs in a typical litter. |
| Giraffe | 18 feet | 1,800 lbs. | A newborn giraffe can be 6 feet tall and weigh 100 pounds. A giraffe's tongue is up to 18 inches long. |
| African Lion | 9 feet | 550 lbs. | A pride of lions generally has 20–40 members. Lions can run up to 37 mph for short distances. |
| Skunk | 30 inches | 6.5 lbs. | Skunks can squirt their musk up to 12 feet. The smell can be detected as far away as a mile and a half. |
| African Elephant | 10–11.5 feet | 6 tons (male) 4 tons (female) | The largest tusk ever recorded was 10 feet long and weighed nearly 230 pounds. |
| Red Fox | 24–42 inches | 10–15 lbs. | Foxes dig tunnels that can be up to 30 feet long, leading to a chamber 3–10 feet below ground. There can be as many as 19 entrances to the tunnel. |
| Black Bear | 3 ft (at shoulder) 5–6 feet long | 250–600 lbs. | Diet is 75% vegetable matter (berries, nuts, roots). |
| Moose | 6–8 feet | 1,300–1,500 lbs. | Moose have a 250-day gestation period. A rack of antlers can span 6 feet. |
| White Rhino | 6.3 feet (height) 12–17 feet (length) | 5,000–7,900 lbs. | White rhinos have two horns on their snouts. Only about 17 are known to exist in the wild, and there are about a dozen in captivity. |

# Big and Small

➤ **Suggested Activity:** In groups of three, one student fingerspells a category, the second student fingerspells the name of the record holder, and the third the corresponding famous fact.

## World Record Holders

| Category | Record Holder | Famous Fact |
| --- | --- | --- |
| Tallest Tribe | The Watussi of Rowanda, Central Africa | Average 6 ft. |
| Smallest Tribe | The Mbutsi Pygmies of the Congo | Men: 4 ft. 4 in.<br>Women: 4ft. 1in. |
| Tallest People | Robert Wadlow, US (male) | 8ft. 11$\frac{1}{10}$ in. |
| | Sandy Allen, US (female) | 7ft. 7$\frac{1}{4}$ in. |
| Shortest People | John and Greg Rice US (twins) (male) | 2 ft. 10 in. |
| | Paulene Masters, Netherlands (female) | 1 ft. 9$\frac{3}{4}$ in. |
| Heaviest People | John Minnoch, US | 1,403 lbs. |
| | Rosalie Bradford, US | 1, 202.24 lbs. |
| Lightest Person | Lucia Xarate, Mexico | 26$\frac{1}{2}$ in. tall; 13 lbs. |
| Smallest Waist | Ethel Granger, England | 13 in. |
| Largest Waist | Walter Hudson, US | 9 ft. 11 in. |
| Heaviest Single Birth | Anna Bates, Canada | 23 lbs. 12 oz |
| Biggest Feet | Matthew McGrory, US | 28$\frac{1}{2}$ size shoes |
| Biggest Gallbladder | 69 year old woman, US | 23 lbs. |
| Heaviest Brain | Brenda Cartwright, US | 5 lbs. 1$\frac{1}{10}$ oz. |
| Lightest Brain | Daniel Lyon, Ireland | 1 lb. 8 oz. |
| Longest Hair | Hu Saelo, Thailand | 16 ft. 10 in. |
| Heaviest Breasts | Eve Lolo, France | 6 lbs. 2 oz. |

# Let's Get Personal

➤ **Suggested Activity:** Go around the room and ask each of your classmates what his/her height is. Record the heights and names. Sort from shortest to tallest.

Example:
| | |
|---|---|
| 4'10" | LeeAnn Smith |
| 5'5" | LaWanda Trubot, Jacob Ivanof, Therese Quendere |
| 6'1" | Marisa Vander Veen, Tyrone Winston |

| Height feet/inches | Classmate Names |
|---|---|
| ———— | ———————————————————— |
| ———— | ———————————————————— |
| ———— | ———————————————————— |
| ———— | ———————————————————— |
| ———— | ———————————————————— |
| ———— | ———————————————————— |
| ———— | ———————————————————— |
| ———— | ———————————————————— |
| ———— | ———————————————————— |
| ———— | ———————————————————— |
| ———— | ———————————————————— |
| ———— | ———————————————————— |
| ———— | ———————————————————— |

# Hot, Cold, Rain, Snow

➤ **Suggested Activity:** With a partner, ask and answer the questions about the weather in the cities listed below.

1. How much snow does Anchorage get in an average year?

2. What is the mean annual temperature for Fairbanks?

3. How much does it generally rain in Seattle in any given year?

4. How much can it rain in Chicago in any given year?

5. How much does it generally snow in Boston in any given year?

6. In an average year, how much snow does New York get?

7. What is the mean annual temperature for Minneapolis?

8. What is the mean annual temperature for San Francisco?

9. What is the average annual rainfall in Denver?

10. What is the average annual snowfall in Washington D.C.?

## Weather Statistics

| City | Mean Annual Temperature | Average Annual Rain | Average Annual Snow |
|------|------------------------|---------------------|---------------------|
| Anchorage | 35 | 15.2" | 69.3" |
| Boston | 51 | 42.5" | 43.1" |
| Chicago | 49 | 31.7" | 39.3" |
| Denver | 50 | 15.5" | 59.0" |
| Fairbanks | 26 | 11.2" | 68.3" |
| Juneau | 40 | 54.7" | 106.4" |
| Minneapolis | 44 | 25.9" | 46.3" |
| New York | 55 | 40.2" | 29.3" |
| San Francisco | 57 | 20.7" | Trace |
| Seattle | 53 | 35.6" | 14.3" |
| Washington, D.C. | 57 | 38.9" | 16.6" |

# Favorite Recipes

➤ **Suggested Activity:** In pairs, one student signs a recipe while the other writes it down. When finished, compare with the original to see if they match. Change roles and repeat, with a different recipe.

---

GRILLED RATTLESNAKE CHINESE STYLE

1 fresh rattlesnake
⅛ cup soy sauce
⅛ cup fresh lime juice
2 tbsp. sweet sherry

Combine the soy sauce, lime juice, and sherry. Cut snake into pieces. Add the snake and marinate for two hours. Prepare a fire in a charcoal grill. Remove the snake from the marinade and keep the marinade. Thread the snake onto bamboo skewers and grill, basting frequently with the marinade until tender.

---

APRICOT LOVE POTION

Combine:
1 cup of apricot nectar
½ cup of seltzer water
1 tablespoon of honey
½ teaspoon of vanilla

Drink while still fizzing. Share with someone you like and see what happens!

---

PLAY DOUGH (Non-hardening variety)

Mix together:
250 ml flour
125 ml salt
10 ml cream of tartar
250 ml water
Few drops of food coloring

In a pan, heat 2 tbsp (10 ml) vegetable oil. Add the mixed ingredients, and cook 3 minutes. Stir constantly. Let the dough cool. Store in plastic wrap in the refrigerator.

# Favorite Recipes—continued

CHOCOLATE CHIRPLE CHIP COOKIES

2½ cup flour
1 tsp baking soda
1 tsp salt
1 cup butter, softened
½ cup sugar
½ cup brown sugar
1 tsp vanilla
2 eggs
10 dry-roasted crickets
1 12-ounce bag chocolate chips
1 cup chopped nuts

Preheat oven to 375. In small bowl, combine flour, baking soda, and salt; set aside. In large bowl, combine butter, sugar, brown sugar and vanilla; beat until creamy. Beat in eggs. Gradually add flour mixture and insects, mix well. Stir in chocolate chips and nuts. Drop by rounded measuring teaspoonfuls onto greased cookie sheet. Bake for 8–10 minutes.

SPICY APPLESAUCE ORNAMENTS (Cinnamon Applesauce Hearts)

1 lb. jar sweetened applesauce
8 oz. cinnamon

Drain jar of applesauce overnight (you will be amazed at how much liquid seeps out). Add cinnamon and mix well. Pat into a ball, pressing hard to solidify and mix. Pat out in 1-cup units onto wax paper. Push to ½" thickness and cut with cookie cutters. . Poke a hole in the top with toothpick. Dry by letting them sit in a warm place for several days, turning them over regularly. When completely dry, hang a ribbon through the hole. Use as a decoration or a sachet. These are NOT edible.

# Calorie and Fat Content

➤ **Suggested Activity:** With a partner, take turns identifying specific candy bars with their calories and fat content by asking and answering the questions below:

1.  How many fat grams are in a roll of Life Savers?

2.  How many calories are in a Mr. Goodbar?

3.  How many fat grams are in a York Peppermint Patty?

4.  How many calories are in an Almond Joy?

5.  How many fat grams are in box of Junior Mints?

6.  How many calories are in a Sugar Daddy?

7.  How many fat grams are in box of Good & Plenty?

8.  How many calories are in a Kit Kat?

9.  How many fat grams are in a Tootsie Roll?

10. How many calories are in a bag of Peanut M & Ms?

## Calories and Fat in Candy Bars

| Candy Bar | Calories | Fat grams |
|---|---|---|
| Almond Joy (1.76 oz) | 250 | 14 |
| Good & Plenty (1.8 oz) | 191 | 0 |
| Hershey's Milk Chocolate (1.55 oz) | 240 | 14 |
| Junior Mints (1.6 oz) | 192 | 5 |
| Kit Kat (1.5 oz) | 230 | 12 |
| Life Savers (.9 oz) | 88 | 0 |
| Peanut M & Ms (1.74 oz) | 250 | 13 |
| Mr. Goodbar (1.9 oz) | 240 | 15 |
| Sugar Daddy (2 oz) | 218 | 1 |
| Tootsie Roll (2.25 oz) | 252 | 6 |
| York Peppermint Patty (1.5 oz) | 180 | 4 |

# Women's Basketball

➤ **Suggested Activity:** With a partner, use the information provided below, to take turns asking and answering the following questions:

1. How tall is Ayanna Brown?

2. How tall is Megan Light?

3. How tall is Chanivia Broussard?

4. How tall is Holli Tapley?

5. How tall is Shelia James?

6. How tall is Amanda Papuga?

7. How tall is Schrene Isidora?

8. How tall is Alicia Hartlaub?

9. How tall is Gail Strumpf?

10. How tall is Meghan Saake?

## Women's Basketball Players

| Cardinal Starters | |
|---|---|
| **Player** | **Height** |
| Megan Light | 5′6″ |
| Holli Tapley | 5′7″ |
| Gail Strumpf | 6′4″ |
| Ayanna Brown | 6′3″ |
| Schrene Isidora | 5′11″ |

| Cougar Starters | |
|---|---|
| **Player** | **Height** |
| Amanda Papuga | 5′10″ |
| Sheila James | 5′5″ |
| Meghan Saake | 5′10″ |
| Alicia Hartlaub | 6′2″ |
| Chanivia Broussard | 6′0″ |

# ► Unit Ten: Fractions

- ❖ **Warm-Up Exercises**

- ❖ **Overview**

- ❖ **Activities:** **Food for Thought**
  **Investor's Diary**
  **When in Rome, or Paris, or Rio . . .**
  **Telephone Game**

# Warm-Up Exercises

**Shoulder Shrugs:** Slowly raise and drop shoulders several times.

**The Swan Dive:** Slowly stretch arms above your head until they meet, palms together. Gently lower them to shoulder level, palms up. Repeat.

**Finger Lifts:** Place hand palm down on a table or flat surface and slowly raise and lower each finger. Repeat with the other hand.

**Full Arm Stretch:** Hold arm out parallel to the floor, palm down. Lock elbow. Raise your hand so the fingertips point to the ceiling. With the other hand, gently press the raised fingers back toward your body for a five-count. Alternate with the other hand. Repeat twice.

**Palm Press:** Press palms together in front of your body. Keeping your elbows high, use the right palm to gently and slowly push the left palm backwards, from the wrist only, toward the left elbow. Slowly and gently, use the left palm to push the right palm backwards, from the wrist only, toward the right elbow. Repeat several times.

**The Frankenstein:** With arms stretched out in front of you, palms down, slowly open and close hands, stretching the fingers apart as far as possible. Repeat several times.

**Wrist Revolutions:** With closed hands, slowly rotate wrists in toward each other several times. Then rotate wrists away from each other several times.

# Overview

### Fractions

The number in the numerator position is signed, followed by a slight downward motion while signing the number in the denominator.

In fractions where both the numerator and denominator are single digits, the palm orientation for the entire fraction depends on the numerator. When the numerator is 1–5, both the numerator and denominator are signed palm in, even if the denominator contains a number greater than 5. However, when the numerator is 6–9, both the numerator and the denominator are signed palm out.

When the fraction is paired with a whole number, the fraction faces the same direction as the whole number. Thus, in 4½, the fraction faces in, because the 4 faces in, but in 7½, the fraction faces out.

### Decimals

The decimal point in ASL is signed using the handshape of a boxed X.

# Food for Thought

➤ **Suggested Activity:** With a partner, determine the serving size and calorie count for 2 servings of each item.

| | |
|---|---|
| Rice Chex<br>Serving Size 1¼ cup<br>Servings per box 16<br>Calories per serving 120 | Enriched Long Spaghetti<br>Serving Size 2 oz<br>Servings per box 11<br>Calories per serving 210 |
| Wheat Thins<br>Serving Size 16 crackers<br>Servings per box 29<br>Calories per serving 150 | Creamy Peanut Butter<br>Serving Size 1¼ tbsp<br>Servings per jar 16<br>Calories per serving 120 |
| Blue Diamond Almonds<br>Serving Size 3 tbsp<br>Servings per can 11<br>Calories per serving 180 | Bittersweet Swiss Chocolate<br>Serving Size 12 squares<br>Servings per bar 2.5<br>Calories per serving 210 |
| Macaroni and Cheese<br>Serving Size 2.5 oz<br>Servings/container 3<br>Calories per serving 250 | Salsa<br>Serving Size 2 tbsp<br>Servings/container 15<br>Calories per serving 10 |
| Basil Rotini Tomato Soup<br>Serving Size 1 cup<br>Servings/container 2<br>Calories per serving 120 | Sourdough Bread<br>Serving Size 1 slice<br>Servings/loaf 18<br>Calories per serving 100 |
| Chopped Broccoli<br>Serving Size ¾ cup<br>Servings per box 3.5<br>Calories per serving 25 | Pulp Free Orange Juice<br>Serving Size 8 oz<br>Servings per can 12<br>Calories per serving 110 |

# Investor's Diary

➤ **Suggested Activity:** With a partner, use the information provided below to take turns asking and answering the following questions about stock prices:

1. What was the change for IBM?

2. What was the high for General Motors?

3. What was the low for Wal-Mart?

4. What was the high for Lucent?

5. What was the low for Disney?

6. What did BellSouth close at?

7. What was the change for Merck?

8. What did Exxon close at?

9. What was the high for AT&T?

10. What was the low for Microsoft?

## Stock Prices

| Stock | High | Low | Close | Change |
|-------|------|------|-------|--------|
| AT&T | 18.25 | 16.50 | 17.06 | −1.88 |
| BellSouth | 41.06 | 39.72 | 40.13 | −.81 |
| Cisco | 40.25 | 35.16 | 38.88 | +2.38 |
| Disney | 27.69 | 26.50 | 27.69 | +.63 |
| Exxon | 86.75 | 84.75 | 84.75 | −.44 |
| General Electric | 48.50 | 47.19 | 47.88 | +.44 |
| General Motors | 52.00 | 48.69 | 51.38 | +1.38 |
| IBM | 87.94 | 80.06 | 81.56 | −4.44 |
| Lucent | 14.56 | 12.50 | 14.19 | −1.31 |
| Merck | 93.63 | 91.00 | 92.50 | −.88 |
| Microsoft | 45.13 | 40.25 | 43.44 | +1.94 |
| Wal-Mart | 52.25 | 49.31 | 51.75 | +2.81 |

# When in Rome, or Paris, or Rio. . .

➤ **Suggested Activity:** With a partner, use the U.S. dollar exchange rate chart for January 21, 2001 to ask and answer questions in the following form: How many *fingerspell currency* can I get for 1 U.S. dollar in *sign or fingerspell country?*

Example: How many *P-E-S-O-S* can I get for 1 US dollar in *A-R-G-E-N-T-I-N-A?*

## Currency Exchange Rates
## (January 21, 2001)

| 1 U.S. Dollar equals | Currency | Country |
|---|---|---|
| 0.97 | Peso | Argentina |
| 1.74 | Dollar | Australia |
| 1.86 | Real | Brazil |
| 0.65 | Pound | Britain |
| 1.45 | Dollar | Canada |
| 7.88 | Yuan Renminbi | China, People's Republic of |
| 7.69 | Krone | Denmark |
| 3.64 | Pound | Egypt |
| 7.49 | Dollar | Hong Kong |
| 3.09 | New Shekel | Israel |
| 114.00 | Yen | Japan |
| 74.76 | Shilling | Kenya |
| 9.39 | New Peso | Mexico |
| 2.16 | Dollar | New Zealand |
| 8.44 | Kroner | Norway |
| 51.52 | Peso | Philippines |
| 7.54 | Rand | South Africa |
| 1,216.00 | Won | South Korea |
| 9.17 | Krona | Sweden |
| 1.58 | Franc | Switzerland |
| 41.17 | Baht | Thailand |
| 673,780.00 | Lira | Turkey |
| 665.00 | Bolivare | Venezuela |

# Telephone Game

➤ **Suggested Activity:** Divide into teams and form lines. The first person in each line faces the instructor; the rest turn around. The instructor signs one of the following items one time only to the front row of students. They then turn and tap the next person in line and sign the same number with context, until the last person has seen the number. That person comes to the front of the line and signs it back to the instructor. Teams with the correct number score one point.

6'3" tall

3:45 am

Social Security number: 311-72-5693

Phone number: (651) 483-1040

2,514 toothpicks

$4,554.99

$50.00 tickets to Rod Stewart

1965 Toyota Tercel

Daily Five Lotto: 8-10-60-25-12

Phone number: 824-9167

$1,489,311 lottery winnings

$1.50 admission

25,406 enrollment at Lansing Community College

¼ of an apple

67 goats

10:15 pm

25 pounds of lettuce

Daily Four Lotto: 5-29-63-22

½ of a pie

33% passed the test

Social Security number: 281-66-6222

2001 Honda Prelude

Zip Code 48864

5'11" tall

Record: 10 wins 3 loses

# Unit Eleven: Ordinal Numbers

❖ **Warm-Up Exercises**

❖ **Overview**

❖ **Activities:** **Take Me out to the Ballgame**
**Peanuts & Crackerjacks**
**Major League Baseball**
**Let's Get Personal**
**Out to Lunch**
**Dewey Decimal Game**

# Warm-Up Exercises

**Shoulder Shrugs:** Slowly raise and drop shoulders several times.

**The Swan Dive:** Slowly stretch arms above your head until they meet, palms together. Gently lower them to shoulder level, palms up. Repeat.

**Finger Lifts:** Place hand palm down on a table or flat surface and slowly raise and lower each finger. Repeat with the other hand.

**Full Arm Stretch:** Hold arm out parallel to the floor, palm down. Lock elbow. Raise your hand so the fingertips point to the ceiling. With the other hand, gently press the raised fingers back toward your body for a five-count. Alternate with the other hand. Repeat twice.

**Palm Press:** Press palms together in front of your body. Keeping your elbows high, use the right palm to gently and slowly push the left palm backwards, from the wrist only, toward the left elbow. Slowly and gently, use the left palm to push the right palm backwards, from the wrist only, toward the right elbow. Repeat several times.

**The Frankenstein:** With arms stretched out in front of you, palms down, slowly open and close hands, stretching the fingers apart as far as possible. Repeat several times.

**Wrist Revolutions:** With closed hands, slowly rotate wrists in toward each other several times. Then rotate wrists away from each other several times.

# Overview

### Ordinal Numbers

Ordinal numbers have two applications: to show order (e.g., the first, second, and third steps in making a stained glass window) and to show position in a series of numbers (e.g., who came in first, second, and third in a race).

To show order, the number twists from palm out to palm in, the fingers remaining in an upright position throughout the movement.

To show position, the number starts palm out, in the regular upright position. The wrist then twists and pulls back toward the body, so the palm faces in, with the fingers rotating into a horizontal position, as shown in the following illustration.

A variant to this second application would be a "throwing forward" of the number. "First," "second," and "third," etc. would be indicated by a sharp bounce of the number, palm left (for right-handed signers) in front of the body.

# Take Me out to the Ballgame

➤ **Suggested Activity:** Using the information in the chart below, with a partner answer the win/loss standings questions for the teams below:

1.  Identify, in order, the top five winning teams.

2.  Identify, in order, the four teams with the worst records.

3.  Identify, in order, the teams that have 90 or more wins.

4.  Identify, in order, the teams that have 85 or more wins.

5.  Identify, in order, the teams that have between 45 and 50 losses.

## NATIONAL LEAGUE STANDINGS

| EAST | Wins | Losses |
|---|---|---|
| Philadelphia | 82 | 40 |
| Atlanta | 79 | 42 |
| Florida | 76 | 46 |
| New York | 63 | 58 |
| Montreal | 58 | 64 |
| **CENTRAL** | **Wins** | **Losses** |
| Chicago | 96 | 25 |
| Houston | 87 | 34 |
| St. Louis | 85 | 36 |
| Milwaukee | 78 | 44 |
| Pittsburgh | 77 | 45 |
| Cincinnati | 70 | 51 |
| **WEST** | **Wins** | **Losses** |
| San Francisco | 91 | 30 |
| Arizona | 89 | 32 |
| Colorado | 75 | 47 |
| San Diego | 69 | 52 |
| Los Angeles | 67 | 55 |

# Peanuts & Crackerjacks

➤ **Suggested Activity:** With a partner, take turns asking and answering the following questions using the statistics below:

1. How many homeruns did the top hitter hit?

2. How many runs did Helton bat in?

3. How many strikeouts did Vazquez have?

4. What were Maddux's pitching wins/losses?

5. What are Sosa's homerun and RBI stats?

## Baseball Statistics

| Homeruns | | Runs Batted In | | Pitching Wins/Losses | | Strikeouts | |
|---|---|---|---|---|---|---|---|
| Bonds | 47 | Gonzalez | 106 | Schilling | 16-5 | Johnson | 259 |
| Gonzalez | 43 | Sosa | 101 | Johnson | 14-5 | Schilling | 205 |
| Sosa | 37 | Helton | 100 | Lieber | 14-5 | Wood | 183 |
| Helton | 34 | Berkman | 92 | Maddux | 14-6 | Park | 167 |
| Green | 31 | Nevin | 92 | Morris | 13-7 | Vazquez | 152 |
| Nevin | 31 | Bagwell | 91 | Dempster | 13-9 | Burkett | 143 |

# Major League Baseball

➤ **Suggested Activity:** With a partner, use the statistics below to take turns asking and answering the following questions:

1. List in order, teams that had more than 2 million people attend home games.

2. List in order, teams that had 1.2 million people or less attend home games.

3. List in order, the top three teams for combined home and away attendance.

4. List in order, which four teams had the lowest combined home and away attendance.

5. List in order, teams that had combined home and away total attendance between 3,000,001 and 3,999,999

## American League Attendance Report

| Team | Home Attendance | Total Home and Away Attendance |
|---|---|---|
| Anaheim | 1,320,125 | 3,196,916 |
| Baltimore | 2,092,256 | 3,634,013 |
| Boston | 1,888,478 | 3,572,461 |
| Chicago | 1,283,895 | 2,837,953 |
| Cleveland | 2,298,895 | 3,831,463 |
| Detroit | 1,406,921 | 2,915,100 |
| Kansas City | 1,055,978 | 2,756,206 |
| Minnesota | 1,303,717 | 2,962,003 |
| New York | 2,423,799 | 4,310,943 |
| Oakland | 1,330,651 | 2,970,778 |
| Seattle | 2,187,467 | 4,041,244 |
| Tampa Bay | 801,743 | 2,440,255 |
| Texas | 1,948,421 | 3,626,852 |
| Toronto | 1,390,479 | 2,788,371 |

# Let's Get Personal

➤ **Suggested Activity:** With a partner, share the following numerical information (real or invented). Be sure to use appropriate ASL structure and grammatical features.

1. Couch Potato:
   - Number of hours of television watching per week?
   - How many channels you get?
   - Favorite channel?
   - Number of video rentals per year?

2. Employment:
   - Work schedule?
   - Length of your lunch break?
   - Office phone number?
   - Fax number?

3. School Days:
   - Age of your first crush?
   - Favorite grade in elementary school?
   - Cost of a hot lunch when you were in high school?
   - Time school started and ended?

4. Cars:
   - Age you got your first car?
   - How much did it cost?
   - Year of your current car?
   - How much did it cost?

# Out to Lunch

---

➤ **Suggested Activity:** Divide into groups of three. Two students act as restaurant patrons, the third as their server. The patrons order from the menu below. The server writes down the ordered items, and then must calculate the final bill for the patrons. The patrons then calculate how much their total is, including a tip.

---

## MENU

APPETIZERS

| | |
|---|---|
| Soup of the Day | $3.50 |
| Fried Cheese | $4.25 |
| Blooming Onion | $4.75 |
| Cheese Breadsticks | $3.95 |

SALADS

| | |
|---|---|
| House Salad | $3.25 |
| Caesar Salad | $5.25 |
| Grilled Chicken Salad | $7.59 |
| Cottage Cheese | $1.40 |
| Taco salad | $4.35 |

ENTREES

| | |
|---|---|
| Spaghetti | $10.95 |
| With sausage or meatball | add $2.00 |
| Filet Mignon | $16.99 |
| Cheeseburger | $4.15 |
| Turkey Club | $4.75 |
| Pizza by the Slice (cheese only) | $1.95 |
| add .35 per topping | |

DESSERTS

| | |
|---|---|
| Apple Crisp | $4.99 |
| Hot Fudge Brownie Sundae | $4.95 |
| Cheesecake | $3.75 |

SIDES

| | |
|---|---|
| French Fries | $1.50 |
| Onion Rings | $2.25 |
| Baked Potato | $2.00 |
| Rice | $1.50 |
| Vegetables | $1.50 |

BEVERAGES

| | |
|---|---|
| Coffee, Tea (hot or iced) | $1.25 |
| Soft Drinks | $1.25 |
| Hot Chocolate | $1.50 |
| Espresso | $2.25 |
| Wine | $4.75 |

# Dewey Decimal Game

➤ **Suggested Activity:** Divide into pairs. Each student takes a different list of Dewey Decimal System numbers for a variety of topics. Ask and answer the following questions using the tables below.

1.  Where can I find books about the teachings of Zen?

2.  Can I find information on tracing my family roots?

3.  I need a cookbook.

4.  How can I find out how to start a hog farm?

5.  Can you show me a travel guide for Paris?

6.  I need details about the fall of Rome.

7.  Where are the books on George Washington Carver's life?

8.  Where can I find information on early settlements in Australia?

9.  I'm looking for my horoscope.

10. I need information on the early warning signs of a heart attack.

## Dewey Decimal System

| 100 | PHILOSOPHY | 900 | HISTORY |
|---|---|---|---|
| 110 | Metaphysics | 910 | Geography & travel |
| 120 | Epistimology | 920 | Biography & genealogy |
| 130 | Astrology, parapsychology & the occult | 930 | History of the ancient world (to ca. 499 A.D.) |
| 140 | Philosophical schools of thought | 940 | History of Europe (ca. 500 A.D. -) |
| 150 | Psychology | 950 | History of Asia |
| 160 | Logic | 960 | History of Africa |
| 170 | Ethics | 970 | History of North America |
| 180 | Ancient, Medieval, & Eastern philosophy | 980 | History of South America |
| 190 | Modern Western Philosophy | 990 | History of other regions |

## Dewey Decimal System—cont'd

| 600 | TECHNOLOGY | | |
|-----|------------|---|---|
| 610 | Medicine | | |
| 620 | Engineering | | |
| 630 | Agriculture | | |
| 640 | Home & family management | | |
| 650 | Management & public relations | | |
| 660 | Chemical engineering | | |
| 670 | Manufacturing | | |
| 680 | Manufacturing specific products | | |
| 690 | Building & construction | | |

# ▶ Unit Twelve: Numbers in Sports

❖ **Warm-Up Exercises**

❖ **Overview**

❖ **Activities:  Sports Scores**
**At the Track: Horse Racing**
**Getting Creative**
**Number Relay**

# Warm-Up Exercises

**Shoulder Shrugs:** Slowly raise and drop shoulders several times.

**The Swan Dive:** Slowly stretch arms above your head until they meet, palms together. Gently lower them to shoulder level, palms up. Repeat.

**Finger Lifts:** Place hand palm down on a table or flat surface and slowly raise and lower each finger. Repeat with the other hand.

**Full Arm Stretch:** Hold arm out parallel to the floor, palm down. Lock elbow. Raise your hand so the fingertips point to the ceiling. With the other hand, gently press the raised fingers back toward your body for a five-count. Alternate with the other hand. Repeat twice.

**Palm Press:** Press palms together in front of your body. Keeping your elbows high, use the right palm to gently and slowly push the left palm backwards, from the wrist only, toward the left elbow. Slowly and gently, use the left palm to push the right palm backwards, from the wrist only, toward the right elbow. Repeat several times.

**The Frankenstein:** With arms stretched out in front of you, palms down, slowly open and close hands, stretching the fingers apart as far as possible. Repeat several times.

**Wrist Revolutions:** With closed hands, slowly rotate wrists in toward each other several times. Then rotate wrists away from each other several times.

# Overview

### Numbers in Sports

Jersey/player numbers are signed palm out close to the chest.

**Jersey Number 99**

Sport scores are signed by indicating the winning score first. This can be done by signing the winning score with one hand, followed by the losing score with the other. It can also be done by using the same hand, starting with the winning score close to the body and the losing score away from the body.

"Home team" (or "my/our" team) and "Away team" (or "their" team) also can be indicated with the close-to-the-body/away-from-the-body movements. The home team score can be signed with one hand, followed by the away team score with the other. You can also do this with two hands, starting with the home team score close to the body and the away team score away from the body.

If the game ends in a tie, both hands are used, signing the score simultaneously while moving from the center of the sign space (close to the body) to opposite sides (right and left).

# Sports Scores

➤ **Suggested Activity:** With a partner, take turns giving the following scores (including team names), as if you are a NEUTRAL observer.

## Basketball

| | | | |
|---|---|---|---|
| Jazz | 99 | Suns | 98 |
| Lakers | 104 | Raptors | 101 |
| Pistons | 102 | Hornets | 97 |
| Pacers | 89 | Magic | 84 |
| Sixers | 103 | Clippers | 92 |
| Bulls | 96 | Nuggets | 93 |
| Celtics | 100 | Cavaliers | 95 |
| Warriors | 92 | Spurs | 88 |

➤ **Suggested Activity:** With a partner take turns giving the following scores (including team names), as if you (the signer) are on the WINNING team.

## Girls Soccer

| | | | |
|---|---|---|---|
| St. Thomas Aquinas | 9 | Miami Lourdes | 0 |
| American Heritage | 4 | Bishop Verot | 1 |
| Douglas | 5 | Spruce Creek | 3 |
| Astronautville | 6 | Cardinal Gibbons | 2 |
| Key West | 2 | Travella | 2 |
| Westminster Academy | 7 | Coconut Creek | 4 |

➤ **Suggested Activity:** With a partner take turns giving the following scores (including team names), as if you (the signer) are on the LOSING team.

## Boys Hockey

| | | | |
|---|---|---|---|
| Grand Ledge | 4 | Saugatuck | 0 |
| Williamston | 5 | Owosso | 3 |
| Portland | 4 | Dansville | 3 |
| Lansing | 3 | Charlotte | 3 |
| Mason | 3 | Holt | 2 |
| Eaton Rapids | 1 | Okemos | 1 |

# At the Track: Horse Racing

➤ **Suggested Activity:** With a partner, use the information provided below to take turns asking and answering the following questions. Use ordinals (first, second, third, etc.) in your answers.

1. If the horses won based on alphabetical order, which horses would win, place, and show?

2. List in order the four lightest jockeys and their weights.

3. List in order the five heaviest jockeys and their weights.

4. List, in alphabetical order, jockeys who weigh 117 or 118 pounds.

5. List, in alphabetical order, jockeys who ride a horse with "Glitter" in its name.

## Horses and Jockeys

| Horse | Jockey | Weight (lbs.) |
|---|---|---|
| Circle's Wish | Coa | 113 |
| Burnham | Nunez | 121 |
| Well Designed | Douglas | 114 |
| Lady Glitter | Sukar | 122 |
| All Best Wishes | Garcia | 120 |
| Glitter Miss | Castellano | 123 |
| Zanny's Dancer | Toribio | 117 |
| Dixie Special | Rivera II | 119 |
| True Glitter | Alcoa | 110 |
| Nautical Nellie | Carlo | 118 |
| Sweetest Secret | Chavez | 115 |
| Shady Lane | Douglas | 118 |
| Bitter Bride | Velez | 112 |
| Carson City Girl | Aguirre | 111 |

# Getting Creative

---

➤ **Suggested Activity:** Create a story to sign for your class incorporating the following numeric topics.

1. Race Announcement:
   - Distance of the run
   - Time the race starts
   - Age group you are in
   - First prize

2. Sports Update:
   - Dates of basketball tournament
   - Jersey number of your favorite player
   - Height of the center
   - Final Score

3. Soccer Program:
   - Number of kids on the team
   - Cost per family
   - Games won-lost-tied
   - Number of teams in the league

4. Girls Basketball:
   - Time the game starts
   - Cost of admission
   - Score at half time
   - Final score

# Number Relay

➤ **Suggested Activity:** Divide into teams and form lines. The first person in each line goes to the blackboard ready to write. The instructor picks a number from the list below and signs it. The first student to correctly write the number on the board wins a point for their team. Students then pass the chalk to the next student in line and go to the back of the line.

5'9" tall

1,301 marbles in a jar

765 fish in a tank

300 sheep

87 plants

25 people

99¢ hamburgers

Social Security number: 812-33-3678

7:23 am

Daily Four Lotto: 12-25-9-33

4½ feet

$8.00 book

1999 VW Bug

50% of people drive black cars

15,681 people at a conference

1:00 pm

Social Security number: 310-29-6776

Phone Number: 930-3225

Daily Three Lotto: 27-16-3

21 years old

6,708,504 condos in New York City

½ inch thickness of a piece of wood

$10,000,000 lottery

6'2" tall

Record: 12 wins 10 losses

Score: 59 to 33

## Numbers 0–10 Illustrations

**0**

**1**

**2**

**3**

**4**

**5**

**6**

**7**

**8**

**9**

**10**

# Numbers 1–10 Illustrations

# Bibliography and Resource List

Bahleda, S. (1996). *Fingerspelling the Real World.* Eagle River, AK: Real World Press.

*Cardinal and Ordinal Systems* [videotape]. (1989). Burtonsville, MD: Sign Media, Inc.

*Fingerspelling and Numbers* [computer software]. (1994). Salem, OR: Sign Enhancers, Inc.

*Incorporating Systems* [videotape]. (1989). Burtonsville, MD: Sign Media, Inc.

*Interactive Sign Language Fingerspelling and Numbers* [computer software]. (1997). Seattle: Palatine, Inc.

*Number Signs for Everyone: Numbering in American Sign Language* [videotape]. (1997). San Diego: Dawn Sign Press.

*Numbering in American Sign Language: Number Signs for Everyone.* (1998). San Diego: Dawn Sign Press.

*Unique Systems* [videotape]. (1989). Burtonsville, MD: Sign Media, Inc.